Praise for Being Heard: Presentation Skills for Attorneys

Faith Pincus provides a comprehensive, well-written road map to mastering the art of presentation skills. From researching the audience, to creating the perfect message, to body language and delivery tips, this wide-reaching book gives you everything you need to know to hit it out of the park in terms of both context and content. Although there is an emphasis on public speaking, the wisdom in this book can benefit anyone preparing for any type of speaking engagement, from a speech to your local homeowners' association to a creative toast at your best friend's wedding to a hardball interview on national television.

—Wendy L. Patrick, JD, PhD, Prosecutor & Media Commentator

What seems at first glance to be yet another primer on effective communication for the inexperienced proves on a closer read to be an extraordinarily useful tool for the old and skeptical as well. Faith Pincus has created a communication toolbox for all of us who struggle with effective oral presentations either all of the time or only some of the time. And she has done so efficiently and effectively in this short, concise, and clear review of practical approaches and reminders for effective communication in both formal and informal settings, whether preparing for oral argument, speaking at a public meeting, or making a short presentation at a club meeting or other more impromptu setting. Faith has compiled suggestions and checklists many of us have used and all too often forgotten or, if new to the arena, simply need to know and use. I am going to put my copy of this book on my reference shelf right next to *The Elements of Style.*

—Hon. C. Kenneth Grosse (Retired), Washington State Court of Appeals

I have observed well over a thousand oral arguments in the California Court of Appeal and I can say, if you are a practicing attorney, read this book. In clear, conversational, and gripping fashion, Faith Pincus demonstrates that presentation skills is indeed an art. How do you cultivate a likeable, confident presence? Which are the most effective methods of delivery? What tools work best for persuasion? What techniques can be used to manage your fears? Pincus answers all these questions and many more. All attorneys, from the uninitiated to the journeyman to the superstar, will benefit from the knowledge and insight Pincus has developed during the past thirty years as a former attorney and presentation skills trainer helping lawyers, CEOs, and executives improve their presentation skills.

—Pablo Drobny, Lead Appellate Court Attorney (Retired 2018),
California Court of Appeal

Faith Pincus, simply put, is both an exceptional speaker and an exceptional writer. She has personally been my coach and mentor for presentation skills and it has been a life-changer! Her book, *Being Heard: Presentation Skills for Attorneys*, is a must-read.

—Joseph E. Ankus, Esq., President/Founder, Ankus Consulting, Inc.

After having the opportunity to preview this book, I was really impressed! This is much more than just another "how-to-do-it" book. There is a wealth of practical information and guidance presented in an easy to locate and easy to read format. It is a compilation of actual experiences of the author and other contributors that sets out how to make presentations that are effective with the audience and enjoyable for the presenter. I wish that the information in the book had been so readily available when I found myself first addressing gatherings, rather than learning through experience.

—Hon. Gilbert (Thad) Gembacz, United States Immigration Judge (Retired)

This is the book I wish existed when I was a young prosecutor and during my thirty-one-plus years as a Senior Writ Attorney at the California Court of Appeal in San Francisco doing CLE presentations. Faith brings her own expertise and experience, as well as that of her many contacts, to create a book that is witty, an easy read, and a bible for any public speaker. It's one I'll now always keep at hand for reference.

—Susan Horst, Of Counsel, California Appellate Law Group,
Former Career Senior Writ Attorney, California Court of Appeal

Faith's book, *Being Heard: Presentation Skills for Attorneys*, is, quite simply, empowering. It takes the anxiety out of the picture. Faith's method is foolproof. She explains what to do, it makes sense, and then you feel empowered to do it. It's a great handbook on presentation skills and it's a terrific, quick read.

—Lisa Peña, Deputy Assistant Secretary, U.S. Treasury Department

Finally, a book with the practical advice and strategies to improve presentation skills! As a public interest environmental attorney, presentation skills is a critical advocacy tool but one that I was never taught or felt particularly confident in. *Being Heard: Presentation Skills for Attorneys* gave me the tools I needed to refine how I prepare and deliver presentations and helped me up my game. There are so many useful tips in here, I continue to go back to it. A must for beginners and more seasoned speakers alike.

—Matt Vespa, Staff Attorney, Earthjustice

Faith's book reads like a conversation with her: fast, engaging, and certain to leave you with at least a few new ideas you will be eager to apply. After years spent observing trials in a busy federal court, those that still stand out are the very few cases in which the attorney compelled the jurors' or the judge's attention not by volume or drama, but by the clarity, relevancy, simplicity, and strength of their presentation. Faith's book has the tools you will need to make sure that whether you are in a courtroom, a boardroom, or at a meeting anywhere in the world, your words will be heard.

—Barbara Barbara Junge, Esq., Federal civil rights attorney,
former civil AUSA and former career law clerk for the late
Honorable William M. Hoeveler, United States District Court,
Southern District of Florida

I am thrilled that Faith Pincus's knowledge and wisdom now exists in this comprehensive publication. The attorneys I work with clamor to attend Faith's in-person program each year—and for good reason, as this book demonstrates. Faith expertly and succinctly covers the practicalities of presentation skills—from organization to the impression you leave on your audience. She also addresses the concerns and roadblocks public speakers face and how to best practice and prepare to avoid them. Beginners and experienced public speakers alike will find something new to take away from this book every time they read it—and every time they prepare to speak. I know I do.

—Angela Inzano, The Chicago Bar Foundation

Faith has written a fun, thoughtful, and most helpful book for anyone who speaks—or needs to speak—in public. The sections for lawyers are full of good advice, and lawyers and others will also benefit greatly from the other public-speaking and media-handling advice she offers. These are truly words *from* the wise!

—Ken Masters, Masters Law Group

Being Heard: Presentation Skills for Attorneys is a must-read for attorneys of all experience levels. Full of sound, practical advice from start to finish, it will put new attorneys years ahead of their colleagues, and even the most seasoned trial attorneys will pick up valuable pointers and understand in a new light lessons already learned.

—Damian Capozzola, Esq., The Law Offices of Damian D. Capozzola, Los Angeles, CA

Presentation skills is something that everybody in law or business has to do. Doing it well is essential to success, but nobody ever teaches you how to do it. Until now. Faith Pincus breaks down the art of successful presentation skills into bite-size chunks. She'll help you analyze your audience, prepare your message, and deliver your talk. She identifies all the common mistakes speakers make and warns you away from them, especially including misuse of PowerPoint. Her best tip: Enthusiasm on the part of the speaker really counts! And if you actually aren't so enthusiastic, fake it.

—Michael Asimow, Visiting Professor, Stanford Law School; Professor of Law Emeritus at the University of California, Los Angeles School of Law

Law school teaches students how to "think like a lawyer." Law school does not teach students how to *speak*. The result is that we can take either side of an argument; and we *may* be effective in a written brief. But, most of our activities are outside the written arena. Our oral skills most often determine how we're seen as leaders, how we attract and keep new clients, and whether we're successful in court, both before the judge and before jurors. In this book, Faith Pincus helps you prepare your message, organize your thoughts, and present your speech. Having made many presentations over the years, I found Faith's work engaging and well worth the reading and rereading. And if you're beginning your career, take serious note. Keep her book by your side when you begin thinking about accepting an engagement to present.

—Ed Poll, JD, MBA, CMC, LawBiz® Management

FAITH PINCUS

BEING HEARD

PRESENTATION SKILLS FOR ATTORNEYS

Cover design by Kelly Book/ABA Design

Printed in the United States of America.

22 21 20 19 18 5 4 3 2 1

ISBN: 978-1-64105-187-3
e-ISBN: 978-1-64105-188-0

Library of Congress Cataloging-in-Publication Data

Names: Pincus, Faith, author.
Title: Being heard : presentation skills for attorneys / Faith Pincus.
Description: Chicago : American Bar Association, 2018. | Includes
    bibliographical references and index.
Identifiers: LCCN 2018028181 | ISBN 9781641051873 (alk. paper)
Subjects: LCSH: Communication in law--United States. | Forensics (Public
    speaking) | Trial practice--United States.
Classification: LCC KF300 .P56 2018 | DDC 658.4/5202434--dc23 LC record available at https://lccn.loc.gov/2018028181

Okay, it seems silly to dedicate a public speaking book, but it may be the only book I ever write, so I'm going to take this opportunity while I have it.

To my cousin Bobby. I miss your jokes.

To my best friend Kitty. Thanks for always being there.

To my Mom, for telling me I could do anything and be anyone I chose. Over and over again. Thanks Mom, you gave me the confidence to do anything and be anyone I chose.

Over and over again.

To my nieces, Sarah, Melissa, Sydney, and Madison. See what Mom said.

Contents

Acknowledgments

It's not the Academy Awards, so I'll try not to go on forever. I just have a few thank-yous to extend.

To my friend Greg Brooks, the most brilliant Public Affairs/Crisis Management expert, and Graphic Artist, I have ever known—thank you for writing the final "Working with the Media" chapter, creating the DVD ad in this book, creating my DVD covers and the graphics that kick off my *Being Heard: Presentation Skills for Attorneys* and *Public Speaking Made Easy* DVDs, and all of your many years of help.

To Honey Amado, Ben Shatz, Robin Meadow, Karen Kimmey, and retired Judge Brian Van Camp—thank you for taking the time out of your incredibly busy schedules to write such great guest chapters specifically related to in-court presentations. To Beranton Whisenant—thank you for your input on our in-court chapters—you are missed. To Grace Brooks— thank you for your witty cartoons and invaluable editing. And to Kevin Theiss, thank you for your terrific editing as well.

To the many judges and justices I interviewed and chatted with over the years—and there are too many to name—thank you for your great stories, your tips for attorneys, and your time.

Tim Brandhorst—thank you for your original faith in me and your feedback and advice for this book. John Palmer, with the ABA—thank you for your subsequent faith in me and your feedback and advice for the book as well.

To everyone who took the time to read this book and provide input as well as your fantastic testimonials—thank you!

And to all of the people—attorneys, judges, justices, and others—who have spoken at my company's Continuing Legal Education seminars across the country, you have my heartfelt appreciation for your time and energy, and sometimes even stories for this book.

Well, I guess I did go on forever. If you actually read this page, thank you as well.

Introduction

This book is a long time coming. I tend to like speaking more than writing, so it took a while. It's based on almost thirty years of experience training various professionals, starting with political candidates and elected officials and extending to attorneys, heads of national nonprofits, executives, friends, and others—as well as my formal education in rhetoric and communication.

It's organized by topic, so feel free to skip around.

However, if you really want to improve your presentation skills, it's important that you do read about each area of public speaking—Audience, Message, and Image/Delivery—otherwise known as my AMI^{TM} method of public speaking.

You need to know about and work on all three to be your best.

You'll find my discussion about knowing your Audience in Chapter Two.

And even if you think all you want or need to do is improve your image and delivery style, it really is critical you read how to organize your presentation, which you'll find in Chapters Three, Four, and Five, all under "Message." Disorganized presentations are one of the biggest problems—and most common mistakes—speakers make. They are also the ones audiences will not forgive, regardless of your delivery acumen.

Chapters Six through Ten will give you skills you need to make your delivery more exciting and captivating—to help you reach your audience.

While almost everything in this book applies to presentations made by attorneys in and out of court (and I point out when my advice does not apply in court), in Part Two I specifically address in-court-related speaking settings.

For the trial level oral argument chapter and the trial advocacy chapter (Chapters 11 and 15), I've summarized insight I've obtained from many judges and justices interviewed for this book, as well as those who have shared their stories and insight with me over the past fourteen years I have had my Continuing Legal Education company.

I've also included three guest chapters by very well-respected attorneys and a retired judge, all dedicated specifically to in-court speaking settings.

And I wrap up Part Two with a bonus chapter on media relations—while not the typical form of presenting we usually think of, it's still a form of communication and presenting your ideas. And these days, it is more important than ever for attorneys to know how to do it.

It would be difficult for anyone to implement all of the ideas in this book (or any how-to book), but try out a few new ones each time you speak, one speech at a time, and you'll improve—each time.

It's a learnable skill after all.

I hope you enjoy it.

Be Heard. This time. Next time. Every time.

PART ONE

THE ART OF PUBLIC SPEAKING

CHAPTER ONE

Why Work at It?

It may seem unnecessary to offer legal professionals advice on how to present information in public. But I'm proposing to do that for two reasons. First, although public speaking is a core skill for anyone in a law firm, there's a big difference between just speaking and really communicating. If you work in the legal field, you can bet that you're going to have to talk to a crowd of people sooner or later. Professionals know that being able to speak well in public has a positive impact on a career. Good public speakers are seen as leaders. And the reverse is also true.

So why not become the best public speaker you can be?

My second reason for writing this book is that I know that I can improve the performance of anyone who has a willingness to learn. I have spent the last thirty years helping attorneys, CEOs, nonprofit leaders, executives, and others improve their presentation skills. I have run seminars, taken part in oral argument prep (and presented oral arguments as well), and privately coached more attorneys than I can remember—both newcomers and old hands—and they all had one thing in common: **They all improved significantly as a result of our work together.**

In the following pages, I have consolidated the most helpful and effective tips of the trade in order for you (and your staff as well) to become better public speakers. These tools have been time-tested and are guaranteed to ensure that both in and out of the courtroom, you project the image and message that you want.

Whether you want to go from good to great, or so-so to good, or even "Jeez, I hate this" to "Okay, I guess I can survive," this book is for you. Simply follow the guidelines I have assembled here and you will be on the road to becoming the public speaker you would like to be.

Let's get started.

My "Friendly" AMI™ Method of Public Speaking

Public speaking is a skill. It is a teachable skill that anyone can learn. This includes people who have never done it before and those who do it all the time but never really learned how to do it right or well. *Everyone* can improve their public speaking, even experienced speakers.

I cover a lot of ground in this book. The most important thing you need to know to follow along and to improve is to utilize my AMI™ Method of Public Speaking. Since we know mnemonics are important, it may help you to remember enough high school French to recall that "ami" is the word for "friend." My method is not only user-friendly but downright indispensable in providing the framework for a winning presentation.

AMI™ stands for "Audience, Message, and Image/Delivery." To improve your presentation skills, and every presentation you give, you must:

- Find out who your AUDIENCE is;
- Craft a careful, organized MESSAGE;
- Present a compelling IMAGE and create a dynamic DELIVERY style to make sure your message gets heard.

This book is organized around those principles:

- In Chapter Two, we start with a discussion about getting to know your audience and getting past the old rules that tend to put up barriers to communication rather than facilitate it.
- Starting with Chapter Three, we move on to a five-step process on how to organize your message.
- Chapter Four gives focused attention on how to create an attention-getting introduction and a memorable conclusion and provides tips on how to make smooth and effective transitions.
- Chapter Five describes several rhetorical techniques that you can use with powerful effect on your audience during a presentation.
- Chapters Six and Seven cover how you can improve your image and your delivery style.
- Chapter Eight provides valuable advice on managing and overcoming fear.

- Chapter Nine is a special break-out on PowerPoint and new technology.
- Chapter Ten discusses how to handle questions during your presentation.

I wrap up the book in Part Two, addressing specific attorney-related speaking situations, such as oral or motion argument (Chapters Eleven and Twelve), opening statements (Chapter Thirteen), closing arguments (Chapter Fourteen), and trial advocacy (Chapter Fifteen). Most of these tips in the chapters are constructive advice and skill-building tips from judges and justices. Some fabulous guest chapters address specific topics just mentioned.

The last chapter in the book (Chapter Sixteen) addresses media relations, including both crisis communication and public relations.

Finally, an appendix in the back of the book contains a handy list of resources.

AUDIENCE

CHAPTER TWO

The Audience Matters

The A of my three-step AMI™ Method of Public Speaking stands for Audience. One of the classic mistakes speakers make is deciding upon their topic and creating their speech without ever considering the wants and needs of their audience. If you think about it, that's a lot like putting on a dinner party for strangers without finding out if your guests have any allergies or dietary restrictions. Before you prepare your presentation, it is imperative that you know who is going to be on the receiving end of it.

Whether you have a specific assigned topic, a vague idea, or no topic at all, you still have to figure out as much about your audience as possible before creating your presentation.

So, your first question should always be: Who will be in my audience? Will I be speaking before a judge, a jury, a room full of attorneys or other professionals at a seminar or conference, a room full of my client's staff forced to attend training sessions, or a room full of potential clients? All of these audiences are different and have different wants and needs, so prepare accordingly.

Your Audience: Six Questions

The first thing to do when preparing your presentation is to find out about your audience so you can tailor your speech to their needs. But where can you get information?

Sometimes it's difficult to get factual background info, but at the very least, you should be able to make an educated guess about the kind of group you'll be speaking to and what their expectations will be. No one is ever asked to speak to a completely unknown audience on a random topic—some information *must* be available to you at the outset: the subject of your presentation, the location of the event, basic background on the audience, and why they are there.

If you have no access to your audience in advance to determine their actual background, then at least look for the answers to these questions:

1. **What is the title of my presentation (if created by someone else)?**—When you are an invited speaker to a training type of event or conference, you may be given the title of the presentation by the event organizers. So make sure you review this in advance, *before* you prepare for your presentation. Besides telling you something about the group's needs, it could keep you from getting blindsided if your prepared speech doesn't fit with the expected message. And sometimes conference organizers will give you a general topic or focus, but then publicize your presentation with a title that doesn't quite match what they said to you over the phone or in email. Believe me, it happens. It has happened to me several times, and now I insist on a solid title before I create my presentation. (I actually rarely let someone else name my presentation—so I insist they use the title I give.)

   By looking at the title in advance (if you didn't create it yourself), you get a picture of what the event organizers want and who they think their audience is. That can be helpful if there isn't any other information upon which to base your presentation.

2. **What is the event?**—Depending on where you are speaking, you'll want to tailor your presentation accordingly. Is this a formal event where you are expected to be more reserved and less casual in your delivery? Are you in front of a judge or jury? Who is the jury? What type of court? Are you providing instructions or running an educational seminar? Are you trying to convince your audience to see a certain topic in a different way? Are you selling something or trying to market an idea or product? Are you speaking at a church about estate planning? Is this a venue that allows for audience-presenter interchange or one that requires the speaker to "monologue"? All of these things, and more, will factor into your preparation, so do your homework.

3. **What is the time of day you will be speaking?**—This vital question is often overlooked. And I'm here to tell you—afternoon sessions are *entirely* different from morning sessions. In the morning, audiences

tend to be well-rested, full of coffee, ready to perk up and listen to you. By 2:30 in the afternoon, once they've spent the morning listening to speakers and had their lunch, half the crowd is likely to nod off if you don't keep the energy percolating. (For that reason, if given the choice, pick the morning slot. You won't regret it.)

4. **What is the nature of the audience?**—No two groups are the same. Audiences come in all shapes, sizes, and persuasions. Thinking of them as a monolithic entity (a "group") isn't going to get you anywhere. So find out: Is it a state bar group? The IP subcommittee? An appellate section? An Administrative Law Judge? Will you be addressing the senior partners at the firm or the new associates? Is it a group of insurance underwriters who may refer business? Laypersons? Doctors? Elected officials? Government personnel? New (or seasoned) attorneys in an international company's corporate law department? How many people are likely to be there? Twenty? Thirty? A thousand? Dig around as much as you can. Surprises are not your friend.

5. **Why are they here?**—Some audiences are going to be friendly, but not all. Find out why this group has been assembled and it will go a long way toward telling you how to make your first approach to them.

   Is attendance at this presentation mandatory? Have they paid to hear you speak? Did they choose to hear you speak, even if they didn't pay (as in a free webinar)? Are you on the agenda because an event or educational planner or partner chose you, or did the attendees help make the decision? Are they there because they have to be? When you are looking at this question, set your ego aside and look at it from the audience's perspective, regardless of your professional reputation.

6. **What benefit are you expected to provide?**—This is key to understanding how to give a successful speech. What exactly do you want to accomplish during this speech? What do you think the audience wants to hear about and walk away with? What will motivate, educate, or activate them, based on their needs? Set a specific goal (e.g., "I want them to have the tools to become better public speakers" or "I want them to understand significant changes in the law" or "I want the judge to have the information she needs to make a decision in favor of my client" or "they should leave with a thorough understanding of . . . "). Then set out to accomplish that goal. Without a goal . . . you're just talking.

Remember, good speeches are about meeting your audience's needs *first*. That's how you excel and how you are remembered. Speakers many times are self-focused instead of audience-focused. But the best speakers focus on the needs and wants of their audience, first and foremost. By meeting their needs, you will accomplish your goals along the way as well.

So set a goal to become one of those types of speakers and you'll already be appreciated more than most speakers.

Seven Audience Types

As you research your audience, you'll want to find out everything you can about them, within the boundaries of what is possible. Here are a few suggestions on how you can connect with seven very different types of audiences. This list is not all-encompassing, there are others of course, but here are a few to get you thinking:

- Judges and justices
- Jurors
- Board executives
- Clients
- CLE or training session attendees in any profession
- Laypersons, community members
- Elected officials

Audience #1: Judges and Justices

The single best way to learn about your judges or justices prior to appearing before them is to take the time to go to the courtroom and sit in on a few arguments. This is best done a week or so before you have your own court appearance. Watching the way they interact with other attorneys will give you a good idea as to the personality and preferences of the judge or justice in front of whom you'll appear. Is this person typically loquacious or quiet? Does he or she make eye contact or avoid the attorney's gaze? You can gain a sense of the judge's or justice's preference for order, format, length of time, and decorum simply by observing him or her in action. And you can gain insight into particular types of arguments, theories, and approaches that a judge or justice favors or disfavors.

And if you happen to be lucky enough that the judge is hearing from an attorney who is arguing a legal point you were also planning to make, then you might strike gold—if the judge rejects or favors that type of legal argument, you now know it going in. (And don't take it just from me—judges make this recommendation to attorneys every time they teach at one of my litigation boot camps.)

Five Ways to Judge a Judge (Or Justice—for the Sake of Convenience, "Judge" Refers to Both Throughout)
Apart from your own personal observation, there are at least five ways to gather helpful background information on a judge:

1. **Seek out colleagues who have appeared before the judge**—They can give you the kind of feedback listed above. You can find them by asking around at your firm, checking out a listserve, or even looking at a bar-related committee upon which you serve—or anywhere else you can think of. Bear in mind that the information you receive will be colored by the attorney's experience (especially whether the case was won or lost), but even so, it never hurts to have a little insight prior to your appearance, even if the opinion is slightly skewed.
2. **Look up your judge**—Use one of the multiple ratings websites or judicial biographical and ratings publications (Leadership Directories and others publish these types of books). This resource is rich in useful information that you should use to your advantage.
3. **Read whatever you can get your hands on that was written by this judge**—Not just articles in trade publications, but the judge's published and, if you can find them, unpublished opinions, especially those relevant to the legal issue(s) at stake in your case/motion. By doing this, you can discover how your judge feels about a specific legal argument in advance and prepare accordingly.
4. **Attend seminars, classes, or events where the judge is speaking or get the recordings**—Watching (or hearing) a judge present is an invaluable way to learn about a judge's preferences, pet peeves, and things that make him or her happy. At these events, judges are usually a great deal less formal than they are in a courtroom setting and are much more willing to open up and provide advice and perspective. It is wonderful how candid judges sometimes are when presenting to attorneys. Usually their goal is to educate

attorneys on how to get it right, so the insight you will receive from that judge—about his or her preferences, perspectives on the law or procedure, and the court in general—is absolutely irreplaceable.

5. **Get to know the judge's bailiff or court clerk**—Ask him or her (in a friendly way, of course) how his or her judge runs motion argument sessions. Avoid personal and political questions for obvious reasons. Some bailiffs or clerks can be cagey or protective of their judges, but a great many of them will be happy to assist you. Don't be shy about approaching these courtroom sources as they, perhaps more than anyone else, know exactly what the judge does—and does not—like to see from the attorneys who practice before him or her.

The more you can find out about your judge, the more you can tailor your argument and your delivery style to meet his or her preferences and needs.

Audience #2: Jurors

In terms of getting information about your audience prior to your presentation, you are obviously a great deal more limited when it comes to juries, but that doesn't mean you are without any resources at all. For example, you have *voir dire* and, in some states, jury questionnaires. It may seem like a cliché, but it's still true: Finding out what magazines people subscribe to, what TV shows and movies they like, and what their hobbies are *will* help you know more about their interests and how they might view a particular issue.

Do not neglect to take every opportunity to learn everything you can about a potential juror. And, most importantly, once you know his or her interests, you can think about what types of stories, analogies, metaphors, and similes will resonate with each individual in your jury. For example, someone using sports metaphors throughout a jury trial would completely lose me if I was on the jury. I don't pay any attention to sports. But if you were to use stories and analogies related to dogs or wine and food, you'd have my attention and—most importantly—I'd get what you were saying.

Do not underestimate the persuasive power of using analogies, metaphors, and stories that track your jury's personal interests.

Again, you are trying to meet your audience's needs and that means communicating with them in a way that they can absorb what you are saying.

There is no question that a person's beliefs (political, religious, moral, etc.) will color the way they think about a particular issue. As much as jurors avow that they will not let their own personal opinions affect their decision making, it is incredibly rare to find jurors who can completely divorce their own deeply held convictions from their opinions in court.

Entire books have been written on the art of jury selection and that is not what I teach, so I won't go on about this any further. I want you to learn about the jurors so you can tailor your message to be more persuasive, based on your jury's interests and beliefs. Someone else can help you improve how you pick your jury.

Audience #3: Business Executives

The executives and board members of a business are generally easier to research. For one thing, you're usually dealing with a smaller number of people than at other presentations, and you will know the names of many or all of them. In addition, board members are very often as familiar with the subject matter of your presentation as you are. And you frequently know them personally.

When speaking to executives you need to find out in advance what they really want and need to get out of your presentation. If you're approaching them with a proposal to form a business alliance with them, for example, you might want to find out how such partnerships have fared in the past. A few calls or emails to a handful of people who will be attending your presentation (or all of them if possible) is a good place to start. If you don't have the ability or access to do this, find the person who does and have him or her do a sample survey of the group for you. If you have contacts on the inside of the company, do what you can to mine as much information from them as possible.

Always read the individuals' bios when you can find them, such as on LinkedIn, and google them to see if there are any recent accomplishments or press articles about them. Do this even if you know them—you never know what you will find. If you have the time, open up separate files on these executives and board members and try to memorize key details about them. Then tailor your message to their interests and concerns. Again, meet *their* needs.

If it is a board you are presenting to, they can be the key decision-makers in a given transaction. Prepare properly for a board presentation and it could be the key to accomplishing your goals or even advancing your career.

Audience #4: Clients

Attorneys frequently make the mistake of walking prospective large clients through long, boring PowerPoint presentations with copious text, complicated graphics, and gratuitous quotes. This is euphemistically called the "dog and pony show." *Do not make this mistake.*

Instead, try a different approach. Take the time to create a good leave-behind that has everything you would have had in your slideshow and whatever else you want a potential client to know about you and your firm.

Then, put your own material aside and concentrate on your potential client. Research the company or individual, of course. You already know this. In addition, if possible, ask for an early tour of the company headquarters or plants, if viewing a potential client's facility would help you understand their business better. Try to compile a list of all the individuals who will be in the presentation and research them, looking for recent press or new projects especially.

On the day of your pitch, give the potential client a brief talk—*without* PowerPoint—highlighting why you or your firm is a good fit. Then, focus most of your time on interacting with your potential client and asking and answering pertinent questions. If you have made it as far as the in-person pitch, chances are they know you're qualified. Concentrate instead on making a connection and showing them where there's a good fit.

Ask any in-house counsel what they are looking for in a pitch meeting and most will say they are trying to figure out if they can work smoothly with the outside firm and its attorneys. Will they be easy to work with? Responsive to the client's particular needs? Do they *listen*? Will they mind the budget? Not go over in-house counsel's head? Will they care about, or pay attention to, the in-house counsel's needs? Is the firm even a good fit, budget- and personality-wise?

These are the types of questions you want to address during your pitch. A good interactive exchange of information between the prospective client and you will be far more productive and impressive than a one-way "dog and pony show." Besides, people like to talk far more than they like to listen, so *get them talking.*

Approach a pitch meeting as you would an oral argument: **A good client pitch should be a dialogue, not a monologue.**

Audience #5: CLE or Training Session Attendees

There is a lot that you can determine about your attendees at these events. And there are strategies that will definitely give you a leg up. I would break it down into the following five areas:

1. Use the Attendance List

Whenever possible, get the attendance list in advance and have your staff (or you) google the attendees (or look them up on the state bar website, in the case of attorneys). Create a list of bios that you can refer to, so you get a general idea of the practice area, type of attorney, level of experience, and so on, of each person scheduled to arrive at the seminar or other training session. Update as you get closer to the presentation and modify your speech accordingly. There is a world of information out there about each of us, especially about professionals in the legal field. *Mine that information and use it.*

For example, before every presentation skills seminar I hold through my CLE company, I have my staff research the attendees. You would be amazed at the information my staff compiles. Not only do they get the usual—year admitted to the bar, type of practice, size of firm if in private practice, and so on—but they also mine information from Facebook and LinkedIn. They give me a lot of background, such as whether attendees have grandkids and are very into family functions; if they like to travel or write; whether they are into sports, animals, or volunteering, and so on; and a variety of other things my staff can find out about each person on the internet.

My staff also always puts a photo of the person, if available, in the bio sheet. That way not only do I have background information about the attendees that I can use to tailor my stories and metaphors, but I also have faces to put with the biographical information and I walk in the door already able to recognize many of the attendees.

While it is hard to do this with an audience larger than about fifty, it is worthwhile to do it when you can.

Example:

Quite some time ago, we were holding our annual Federal Court Boot Camp in Miami and one of the speakers, a thirty-plus-year career law clerk for a district court judge, asked for the attendance list and then took the time to google all of the attendees.

Now, normally our Federal Court Boot Camps (held all over the country) draw an audience that is 80 percent newer attorneys and 20 percent more experienced attorneys who are either new to Federal Court or need a refresher course because they usually practice in state court. But what Barbara, the speaker, discovered at this particular program, and for the first time ever, was that 50 percent of the audience were experienced attorneys. She even knew some of them personally and one was a judge. Barbara promptly let all the other speakers on the panel know and they were able to adjust their presentations accordingly. Now you might be asking yourself why my CLE company didn't provide that information.

Well, in a perfect world, we would. But we put on fifty or so seminars a year in four states and simply don't have the time or resources. That's why we give the attendee lists to the speakers. Most CLE companies and bar associations operate the same way.

2. Put Together a Survey

If possible, ask the program organizer to email a two- to three-question survey to the attendees in advance, so you can get more information about them and tailor your presentation to their needs. Ask the organizer to either send you the attendees' responses or provide your email address in the survey for a direct response back to you.

If you get permission to contact the attendees in this way, be sure to ask simple, short, and quick-to-answer questions. For example, when I have done this I ask things like:

- "How much public speaking experience do you have?" Options are none, some (every one or two years), moderate (two to four times per year), or extensive (more than five times per year).
- "What would you most like to get out of this program?"
- "What type of speaking do you do?"
- "How often do you speak in public?"

And that's it. Once you get the answers to very simple, easy-to-answer questions, you will know an extraordinary amount of information about your audience before you even set foot in the room.

3. If You're Flying Blind, Improvise

If you can't do the above, then ask the program organizer to give you as much information as possible about the particular audience they expect, or, at the very least, ask them to describe the usual audience they get at this function/event. Any information, no matter how trivial, can be made useful in your presentation.

4. Arrive Early and Interact

When speaking at a CLE or other training program you also always want to **arrive early and meet and greet.** This is one of the *most* important things you can do and one of the techniques used *least* often. Whenever possible, arrive fifteen to thirty minutes in advance and introduce yourself one-on-one to as many audience members as possible (regardless of the size of audience). Ask them why they are there and what they are hoping to learn from the program.

What does this do for you? First, it gives you more information about your audience, or a sample of them, so that you can tweak your presentation at the last minute (as needed) to better meet their needs.

Second, it helps break the ice with your audience. It will remove the speaker-audience barrier and make you seem more human and approachable.

Why does this matter?

Because the more familiar you are to them, the more responsive your audience is going to be to you. They will like you and respect you far more than if you come into the room with an air of distance, or worse, superiority. If they think you're talking down to them or that you, God forbid, think you're better than they are, they will reject your message before they even hear it. You can avoid that impression from the get-go if you say hello one-on-one and ask attendees about themselves.

This is where I'm supposed to connect with my audience. So everyone yell out your favorite color. That should do it.

True story:

I was recently having dinner with attorneys at the end of the day of an annual State Bar convention. I knew some of the attorneys and others I did not. During dinner, the topic moved on to public speaking and one of the attorneys stated that he believed speakers should always hold themselves above their audience in order to be credible. He specifically said there should be distance and a certain amount of "I'm better than you" condescension by the speaker.

I could not move him off this belief, despite his knowledge of my background (and his lack of public speaking expertise). I was astonished to hear someone say something so blatantly wrong and with such conviction, especially since his advice was simply disastrous.

Just to be clear: you do not want to hold yourself above your audience, nor do you want to be condescending. Unless you want the audience to hate you, that is. In that case, go right ahead.

5. Network First

Pretty similar to #4 just mentioned, do not, under any circumstances, just walk on up to your podium or panel table and sit there ignoring your audience until you begin speaking. Despite my saying this, I know a lot of people are going to continue to do just this.

The funny thing is, if you spend time briefly meeting your audience one-by-one, before you speak, not only do you accomplish everything I point out above, you also begin to create relationships that will make your speaking engagement far more valuable from a business development and relationship-building perspective than had you just shown up, trotted to the podium, and waited, silently, to speak.

Instead, reach out to your attendees—make yourself known to as many people there as possible. Let them get to know you as both an expert and a nice person. These professionals will be much more inclined to consult you and/or refer business to you if their first contact isn't just as an anonymous person in a conference room chair. And if you are in private practice, meeting people at these functions and getting referrals is usually one of the primary reasons you are speaking at a training program to begin with (in addition to service and other more altruistic reasons).

Even more interesting to me, as an owner of a large CLE business, is the fact that the speakers who are most likely to take my advice at our

Pincus Pro Ed CLE seminars are court staff attorneys and judges, none of which stand to get clients out of the speaking engagement.

> ### Another True Story:
> Once at a program in Florida one of the recently retired state judges even started doing card tricks with a small group of the audience while waiting for the program to begin. It was hilarious. He was good at it, and they enjoyed the interaction very much.

Last point on this subject: These tips are useful whether you are speaking alone or on a panel. In fact, when you are on a panel, it is even more important that you spend time connecting with your audience before the program. If, instead, you sit up at the table and chat only with your fellow speakers, you are strengthening a perception of "us" versus "them"—speakers versus audience. It probably won't offend your audience, because that's what they are used to, but it certainly won't help you connect with them.

So be different. **Surprise your audience.** Introduce yourself to a few of them one at a time; shake their hands; *and* remember to get some piece of information that will help you fine-tune your speech on the fly to even better meet their needs.

And if you can mention one or two of the audience members during your presentation to show that you remembered them, they will never forget you.

Audience #6: Laypersons, Community Members

This type of audience is generally the hardest to research ahead of time, so your best option is the same as #5 (CLE or Training Session Attendees) and for the same reasons. Try as many as you can of the options listed under "CLE." This will depend upon your venue, the organizer, and advance registration. The early arrival, the meet and greet, the early interaction . . . all of these can make your presentations to strangers go that much smoother.

If you're a solo or small firm practitioner using public speaking as a business development tool, such as speaking at a church or community event, the approach related to meet and greet and networking, under Audience #5, is critical.

Audience #7: Elected Officials

When talking to a city council or other governmental board, go beyond the usual. Don't just find out to what political party your audience subscribes. That isn't going nearly far enough. Find out if they are up for election, what projects they have voted for (and why), and what they have voted against (and why). Who are their supporters or detractors (if they have any)? Read everything they've ever written and published. Check their website to see what they claim their positions are on any issues that affect your client or cause. What have they said publicly?

You may also have the opportunity to watch the elected official in board/council meetings on your local TV cable channel. For example, the Sierra Madre City Council in California televises all of its council meetings that are open to the public. You can get a good sense of their public persona, how they treat people speaking in front of them, and how they get along with—or not—their fellow council members.

Use these types of opportunities to find out what the relationships and tensions are between the members, so you are at least aware of any potential traps. Find out which of their constituencies are most vocal and be prepared to address any issues that come up related to your topic if connected to those constituencies.

Government boards see a lot of presentations—*most of them bad.* They listen to bad speeches with boring PowerPoint slideshows in them all day, every day. Your job is to be the memorable speaker—the bright spot in a dreary lineup.

Make a successful, interesting, and memorable presentation to a group like this—and one that meets their needs—and they won't just be grateful, they'll be eating out of the palm of your hand.

Audience = People

These examples of how to talk to CLE attendees, judges, and other audience members are some tips and practices that have worked for me over the years. Sometimes, these ideas have come from the horse's mouth, as it were—as I mentioned, judges are the ones that gave me the best information about how to research judges (and justices). But all of these tips underscore the same point: Don't fall into the trap of disregarding your audience or taking them for granted. They are the first part of the three-step AMI™ Method to deliver a more successful speech. Find out what you can. Strategize how to engage. Go to a little more effort to make a connection.

And once you've considered who you're speaking in front of, it's time to begin some serious thought about building your presentation from the ground up.

MESSAGE

CHAPTER THREE

Create a Memorable Message

Be Brilliant at the Basics

Remember my "friendly" AMI™ Method—Audience, Message, and Image/Delivery? Not hard to figure out that having spent some time talking about who you'll be speaking to, we're going to concentrate now on the M—your Message. And to kick it off, I'd like to start with a joke: A funny thing happened on the way to writing this book . . . I coached hundreds of attorneys, executives, politicians, and nonprofit staff members.

Okay, that's not really funny. (As I confess later on, I'm not a born joke-teller.) What *is* funny is that when a client requests time with me for one-on-one coaching, or even in a small group setting, they always say they don't need help with their organization, just their delivery. Every . . . single . . . time.

And what I'm going to say next is very predictable: **I've *never* met a client who didn't need to work on his or her speech organization.**

Everyone needs help with creating and organizing their message. This isn't a bad thing; it's a true thing. And it also means that you really, really shouldn't skip this chapter. (Not that you'd skip *any* chapter, right?)

The reason attorneys trip up when organizing their presentations is that most people taught in law school have never been *trained* to create speeches.

For some reason, a lot of folks think that the basic rules of essay writing don't apply to creating a presentation. But they do—at least for most presentations, and definitely for legal and business presentations.

- Yes, you really do need an introduction, a conclusion, and a body in your speech.
- Yes, you really do need transitions.
- Yes, you really do need main points and sub-points that logically flow, even if those sub-points are simply examples or explanations.

Organizing all that isn't just daunting—it sounds *boring*. Too bad. If you want to deliver an effective speech, you have to buckle down and deal with the hard work of organizing your presentation in the first place.

Four Types of Speeches (and the One on Which to Concentrate)

One fine day I was chatting with someone who happened to state that he was terrible at extemporaneous speaking: "all that last-minute stuff and such." Whoops! Okay, I know I'm a speech geek, but this is important. Before you can learn to be a better presenter, we have to get some vocabulary straight. "All that last-minute stuff and such" is called *impromptu* speaking, not *extemporaneous*, and there is a very big difference.

What types of speeches are there, you ask? The most common are:

- Impromptu
- Extemporaneous
- Written out verbatim (word-for-word)
- Delivered from memory (usually written out, then memorized).

In the anecdote above, my friend was confusing extemporaneous speaking with impromptu speaking—a common mistake. So let's look at these forms of speaking a little more closely.

Different Presentation Methods, Different Results

Impromptu. This is exactly what it sounds like. It's when someone asks you at a meeting to give a report about something and you didn't know that request was coming—you haven't pre-prepared a presentation. It's when you decide at the very last minute to give a toast at a friend's wedding without any prior preparation or thought. It's when someone at an event decides to invite you to the podium to say something about someone and you didn't know the request was coming. It's what I call "last-minute speaking." Or, as some of my clients liked to do before they met me, "winging it."

I had a third point but I've forgotten it, so I'm taking suggestions.

Extemporaneous. This is where you prepare an outline or speaking notes. You do not write out your presentation word-for-word. You plan and prepare your presentation in advance to the extent to which you know what you are going to discuss, what examples you plan to use, what stories you want to tell, etc. And you have the critical phrases, words, and notes needed to keep you on track and jog your memory written in your "Keyword Outline" (which we'll cover in more detail later on). When you speak extemporaneously, you are prepared. But because the speech isn't written out, you can deliver it in a conversational, polished style without sounding like you are reading a speech.

In most circumstances, extemporaneous speaking is the best form of presentation style. It allows you to adapt to your audience, make eye contact, and have a strong, competent delivery style, yet you have prepared enough in advance that you stay focused, on track, on time, and you present in an organized, easy-to-follow fashion. This is especially true in speeches where persuasion or motivation is all-important, as it often is in business and legal presentations. This extemporaneous style is used less in high-level political speaking, where every word is analyzed over and over and over again and the speeches are written by someone other than the speaker.

Written out word-for-word. Yep, it's just what it sounds like. You write out your speech verbatim and then in most cases, you read it. But repeat after me: There are very few people who can read a verbatim speech well, and they usually have teleprompters. It may sound like an attractive option if you have a little stage fright or are worried about saying anything wrong. The problem with it is that it makes it almost impossible to really connect on a human level with your audience—it tends to result in a very stiff and unnatural delivery, and sometimes people will tune you out. So unless you're running for president and have a teleprompter, I don't recommend this route. But if you are, and you are using a teleprompter, be sure to practice using it with your speech so you don't flub up.

Memorized. Some people like to write their speech out word-for-word then memorize it. It's a risky technique and I've only ever seen college-level speech and debate students do it well. Even then, it usually sounds stilted and overly rhythmic. The only advantage to this method is that you might cut down on your um's and uh's, and, in theory, you will have included everything you want to say in your speech. But it leaves you open to the dangerous possibility that once you begin, the memorization fails you. In that case, you're often worse off than if you were totally unprepared.

And there are other negatives to this approach:

- You can't respond to questions during your presentation without risking getting off track or forgetting.
- You can't make last-minute changes based upon last-minute knowledge you gain about your audience or happenings at the event.

- As with the verbatim speech above, it's hard to deliver without sounding stilted.
- Unless you're twenty-two, or Erwin Chemerinsky, it's pretty hard to memorize a speech if it's more than a few minutes long. So you end up not discussing everything you want to say after all.

For those reasons, I do not recommend the memorization method. I do, however, recommend that whatever presentation method you choose, you make yourself so totally familiar with your introduction and conclusions that they are in effect memorized (more on that later).

To summarize, to improve your speaking skills, focus on creating extemporaneous speeches, since that is the most common and most effective method of delivery for most people. Build an effective speaking style based on prior preparation and practice, which is the focus of this book. But don't forget about impromptu speaking—you'll find a few tips here and there about impromptu speeches later on.

Developing your message is about content *and* organization.

I have a simple five-step process you can use to create your presentation in an organized manner. It may even remind you of college. But its simplicity is its beauty—it is a *never fail* system.

Step 1: Create a Thesis Statement

Your first step is to decide the purpose of your presentation, preferably in relation to your audience's needs. Here, you set your goal. You articulate your goal when you create your thesis statement.

Your thesis statement should be a short descriptive sentence. It's not something you're going to say to your audience necessarily; it's something you are going to use to *guide the creation* of your presentation.

To be clear: I'm not talking about your motivation for speaking, like business development or because a partner or client requires it, or because it's your job. I'm talking about your *presentation's* purpose, for example:

- Are you there to educate your audience about a topic—a new legal theory or case, a skill, a law?
- Are you there to persuade a jury to rule in favor of your client, or a judge to grant your motion?
- Are you trying to convince a potential client to hire your firm?
- Are you trying to accept an award graciously and with meaning?

- Are you there to teach your associates about business development or give them a case update or train your client's staff on company policies or government compliance?
- Is it a wedding toast? Or a business or politically related roast of an individual?

Ask yourself what do you want to accomplish with your presentation, based upon your audience's needs and the occasion for the presentation? Take a minute to think about it first and it will save you grief and work later. If you have gone through the process from Chapter Two of considering your audience, you may already have thought through some of this. Considering what your audience wants may give you a boost in figuring out how to craft the perfect message.

Once you've settled on your purpose, *write it down*. This is your speech thesis. Everything that happens afterwards is the result of taking this first step.

Practice Tip:

When you have finished creating your entire presentation outline, always go back to your *written* thesis statement and make sure your presentation accomplishes the goal you articulated in your thesis statement.

Step 2: Research and Gather Supporting Materials

(As a quick aside, the third step of the process will be condensing your materials into three main points. I mention it here because that step is interchangeable with Step 2. Keep it in mind: After reading both, you may decide you want to put Step 3 first.)

Just as a culinary masterpiece begins with the best ingredients, crafting a great speech begins with getting the best supporting material you can and knowing what you can do with it. Even if your planned speech is something anecdotal or casual, you will want to give some real thought to what is going into your particular "soufflé" and how you can get the best results from it. In this step of the process, you gather together the information you plan on using to communicate your message. It's worth spending some time on it. Here's how I'm going to divide things up:

- **Hard data**—Facts, case studies, and statistics
- **Soft data**—Anecdotal/fictional touches such as:
  - Stories and anecdotes
  - Quotes, articles, and interviews
  - Real and rhetorical questions
  - Humor
  - And even props
- **Legal material**—
  - Deposition, hearing, or other testimony
  - Cases, statutes; legal opinions.

I finish up by reviewing everything in an abbreviated way to help it stick with you.

Hard Data

Maybe it goes without saying, but the two important things about your factual data are that it be (a) accurate and (b) relevant. There's no point in reaching for mathematical support for an argument if even a child can figure out that your numbers don't add up. And there's no point in reaching for impressive statistics from a world-renowned organization if the information really doesn't help make your case. Besides that, here's what you need to know about how to handle this kind of information to give your speech maximum impact:

Facts

Keep facts simple, clear, and organized. Whatever you do, don't overwhelm your audience. If you flood them with a tidal wave of facts, they will not be able to hear or absorb them. Facts are best told, and easiest understood, through stories.

Statistics

My advice for the body of your speech is the same as it is for the introduction: When it comes to statistics, don't use too many of them. Use as few as are necessary, and use them to drive your point home, not to make your point for you.

Additionally—round off. Don't use super detailed statistics. Use analogies or metaphors to make them understandable. Cite your source to make them credible.

> **Tip:**
> For maximum delivery effect, state three statistics in a row, getting slightly louder with each one, then repeat the most important one.

If you find yourself having to present reports with lots of numbers, you'll need to use an even lighter touch. Unless you're speaking to a very unusual audience—remember the all-important Audience part of the AMI™ Method from Chapter Two—chances are people will not respond to a lot of numbers and dry, factual material. And if they can't take it in, they can't process it or retain it and it does nothing to solidify your message.

My best advice, if your presentation requires a lot of hard data: Instead of citing endless statistics, budget figures, or company policy (and slowly boring your audience to death), pick the highlights. Choose only the data that is worth mentioning, discussing, celebrating, or explaining. Put the rest in a "leave-behind" report so everyone can read it and process it on their own time. Your audience will thank you profusely for your thoughtfulness.

When possible, have a story or example to go with each statistic, so you're not just reading them aloud from the podium. Presume your audience can read as well as you can and then give them a reason to want to listen to you instead.

> **One Last Tip:**
> When using statistics or numbers, especially startling ones, *use repetition to drive the point home*. For example, when I talk about how long it takes to make a first impression, I state the number . . . pause . . . drag it out . . . repeat it again more slowly and a little bit louder, then I say it again as a full sentence.

Soft Data
Stories
We live in a world where stories are used to communicate messages. People spend a large majority of their time watching, reading, and listening to stories—on TV, at the movies, on the internet, in blogs, and in the ever-vanishing print media. We grow up being told stories (and telling our children stories) in order to learn values, ways to behave, history, and other things.

Since storytelling is how we are conditioned to learn early on, and how most people like to hear and learn about things, be sure to employ it in your presentations as well.

Stories make us happy or sad or livid and can evoke a hundred other emotions. Stories are communication tools that allow our brains to absorb a lot of information that might otherwise be too difficult to comprehend. Even if you can't articulate your reaction to a story, you can feel it viscerally. That is what makes stories so powerful.

To find common examples of this, go to your local newspaper. Listen to your kids talk about school. Talk to your assistant or colleague at work about his or her weekend. Everything you hear will be told to you in the form of a story. That is why storytelling is such an essential part of almost any presentation. So how can you make it work best for you and your presentation?

As you come across stories you like and think you might find useful later—of your own or told by others—get a "story" file going. I keep mine in Evernote, a cloud application that lets me access them anywhere. It's impossible to remember every story you hear, so write them down for later use.

Then hone the art of storytelling and use that skill as often as possible. I recently discovered a game called "The Storymatic.®" I recommend picking it up and using it as a practice tool to develop your storytelling skills.[1]

Like anything else, the more you practice, the better you'll get. Take note of the communicators—speakers, advertisers, and even comedians— that you think have the most effective delivery and try to analyze why their methods are working.

Anecdotes

Anecdotes are defined as short, amusing stories, usually about real incidents or people. When they're told from personal experience, they have an added benefit of humanizing the speaker. But because of that personal aspect, you should be careful of overdoing it with anecdotes. Be a hard editor: Does

---

[1] "The Storymatic.®" is a game. You are given two cards. The first has two words describing your character. The second has two words or phrases describing a setting or event that must be used in the story. You must create (and tell out loud) a story that uses the character and incorporates the setting/event words. When using it for practice, try to create something that paints a picture of the story you are trying to tell. Give yourself a bit of time to work with it. Creating a story out of whole cloth is not an easy thing to do unless you are experienced at it.

this anecdote really improve my presentation, or is it just one that I like to tell? Does it build up my message, or does it just present me in a flattering light? There's nothing wrong with building your own credibility with your audience, but if you find that you can't edit your anecdote to keep it short, you should think about living without it.

I go into the entire subject of humor later in this chapter, but for now, it's enough to say that the most basic rule with stories and anecdotes is that they need to be relevant, interesting . . . and *short*.

Examples and Explanations

Examples and explanations are another communication tool in your "supporting material" arsenal. Unlike stories, however, examples and explanations do not require a beginning, a middle, and an end. They simply need to be plain statements to clarify a specific point.

What is the difference between an example or explanation and a story? Example of a story: A young boy walks to school, gets distracted by a beautiful pond, decides to go fishing, and misses his final exam. It has a subject, a storyline, and, if told properly, a moral.

In contrast, an example or explanation is offered to illuminate a point. If you're talking about poor decision-making, you might reference buying a name-brand watch from a street vendor or going out partying the night before an exam. These are examples, but they aren't stories. There's a distinct difference.

When using an explanation to support a point, be sure to be clear and brief. Some speakers get in trouble when they begin explaining a concept and then start to meander down various roads that aren't really related to the concept they started out explaining. I call it going down a rabbit hole.

Stay focused on the point at hand and cut out peripheral information that relates to a different point, whether it's similar or not.

The beauty, and challenge, of creating a presentation is to keep it on point, organized, and focused so that you accomplish your purpose. This is actually harder than it sounds because most people have a lot to say about a great number of topics, and especially about their favorite topic or their area of expertise. As a result, many speakers get in trouble because they include all sorts of extraneous information that they find interesting even when it's not necessary.

As a quick aside, if you've been paying attention, you might have noticed that the advice on stories, anecdotes, examples, and explanations has a similar bottom line: *Be brief, stay on point.* These can be great tools to communicate your message, but if you let them get away from you, your audience may leave remembering your anecdote but not why you told it.

Quotes

Quotes are like stories. They communicate ideas, concepts, morals, lessons . . . Best of all, you don't even have to think them up yourself. Just go to a great quote website (or even, *gasp*, an old quote book) and look under your topic/ key words to find something that will help you communicate your point. You'll find a list of quote websites and helpful books in the appendix.

A word to the wise:

Do a little bit of homework if you're taking a quote from the internet. Check on the source, the quote, the context. Do a little quick checking of the source, if you don't know him or her. As rich a resource as the internet is, it is unfortunately too easy to find quotes that are either of questionable origin or from questionable sources. And many quotes attributed to famous authors are ascribed to them incorrectly, or are mis-worded from the original quote.

If you have a famous quote, to be absolutely certain of its wording and attribution, check to see if it is in *Respectfully Quoted, A Dictionary of Quotations*, which I mention in the appendix. This book has more than 20,000 quotes verified by the staff at the Library of Congress.

Make sure to keep your quote simple and directed to your point. If it's brilliant but would be over the heads of your audience, consider para-phrasing to get the essence of it – but note that you have done so.

Personally, I use quotes in my introductions and my conclusions more than in the body of my presentation, but they can also be useful to help communicate any one of my points. Another advantage of quotes is that they lend your presentation an air of authenticity. After all, if Thomas Jefferson agrees with you, who is your audience to argue?

Articles

For the purposes of a speech, taking material from a print, audio, or video product is a lot like using a quote. After all, you can hardly present the entire magazine article or documentary. Lifting a specific part can be a good way to relate a lot of information in a power-packed, abbreviated form, especially if you have reason to believe that your audience is familiar with (and has good associations with) the original context.

You can, when necessary, use opinion-type article sources as long as you are careful that your source matches your audience's belief system to a certain degree. For example, you don't want to be quoting a blog written by Rush Limbaugh to a meeting of the Young Democrats and you don't want to quote Jon Stewart to members of the Tea Party (unless you are making an intentional comparison or joke, that is).

Besides that, when you're using articles, remember to:

- Use a credible source—one that has authority on the subject both to people generally and to your audience specifically.
- If possible, use a source that is known by your audience, at least in name or concept.
- As with quotes, stick to what is understandable—i.e., keep it simple.
- Keep it short and to the point.
- Cite the article properly. Don't reference the wrong author or publication.

Interviews

Interviewing people is an excellent way to get specific, tailored quotes to support your points. Because of the extra effort and the element of uncertainty about results, speakers don't always think of getting an interview to give them material, but that's why it offers some fresh possibilities and can liven up a dry part of your presentation. Be sure that you take the time to do this in advance so you have plenty of opportunity to transcribe the interview and review your notes in order to pick out the right quotes and information to use. Also, in some circumstances you should get permission from the person interviewed to use quotes from the interview.

Real and Rhetorical Questions

You may want to consider questions as elements to include in your presentation. These are the ones that you—the speaker—would pose. These might be things where you really do want people to weigh in, for the sake of audience involvement or confirmation. Or else they can be questions that you ask and then answer yourself. It's a way to address areas where you feel that there are natural thoughts or concerns that arise.

Questions divide into two camps: rhetorical and real. Rhetorical questions are those asked just for effect, and an answer isn't expected (e.g., "But who's counting?"). When using a rhetorical question, be certain to pause and make eye contact with your audience only so long as to make the point and let them think, then move on. If you pause too long, they may begin to wonder if you are expecting a response.

Rhetorical questions are effective in most types of presentations, including opening and closing arguments. Be wary of using them in oral argument as you risk irritating the judge, who wants you to answer his or her questions, not to be peppered by rhetorical ones from you.

Real questions are just what they sound like: questions that either have an answer or open up a line of inquiry. For real questions, it works best if you keep them short and to the point and if you *tell your audience the method by which they should answer them.* You want to give your audience permission to shout it out, raise their hand, or write the answer down for later or discuss it in a group. Without your direction, they might assume your question is rhetorical or they might be too embarrassed to answer. Cue them to respond and, generally speaking, they will.

Humor

We discuss humor in more depth in the section "What Should Go into Your Introduction?" in Chapter Four. For this gathering and research phase, it's enough to say that humor certainly has a place in a good speech *if* it is relevant, it won't be offensive to your audience, and you are good at telling funny stories. Obviously, having something humorous in your presentation isn't essential (unless you're the keynote speaker at a clown college), so don't include it unless you're sure it is working for you.

If you have a good joke or anecdote, it can be an effective addition. If you're using one in an introduction, it will work better if the joke has some connection to your presentation topic or purpose. This means that your joke—in addition to being funny, being told well, and not being offensive—needs some moral center, some relevance.

If you want to add in some humorous elements and don't know where to get them, that may present a more difficult challenge. The best material is fresh, so looking in anything along the lines of a joke book probably won't work. There are certainly online sites that are devoted to humor, but many of the jokes will likely be putdowns at best or questionable material at worst. If you see something funny on a show, movie, or stand-up act and want to give it a try, you could research it to get the words right—you can find almost anything online somewhere—and include it, with the proper accreditation. But you may find that it's just not coming off well. Comedians and actors work hard to get their delivery down pat, and even then, they may have the advantage of getting to do a second or third take.

You won't have that luxury, so my advice is to perform any joke or story you're not sure about for a friend or staff member and ask for their *honest* critique. If you can't do it well, don't do it at all.

In any case, remember to add humorous touches lightly. An over-reliance on them can make you look, quite literally, as if you're not serious about your subject. And it is hard to recover from a joke that goes wrong.

Legal Materials

Cases

This may be self-explanatory but can't go without mention: There are a few specific rules to remember when using, or citing, a case in a presentation.

1. Always state the case name twice if you're going to cite it at all, as in "Jones v. Acme Corporation, 25 U.S. 409 . . . that's Jones v. Acme Corporation, 25 U.S. 409." Repetition reinforces your point, and most people won't get it on the first round if they are taking notes or want to write it down.

2. Instead of, or in addition to, citing the case, be sure to provide your audience with a printed list of case names, citations, and jump pages related to your discussion either before or after your presentation. Be sure to tell your audience they have, or will have, this resource, so they understand why you are not verbally citing the case.

   Caveat: When you need to make a clean record—for example, at a motion argument—fully cite the case. Do it clearly, slowly, and state it twice to make sure the court reporter got it right and *always* give the court reporter a list of the cases you'll be citing before your argument.

3. Never put a citation up on a PowerPoint slide. They are impossible to read and invariably someone in your audience will shout out "Wait!" when you change slides because they haven't copied it all down. See rule #2 above instead.

Deposition, Hearing, or Other Testimony

Using deposition or hearing testimony, like a case citation, needs little explanation. As with cases, there are a few basic rules for its use in a presentation.

First, pick out what portion of the testimony you need to communicate your message and nothing more—or less. Selecting too much can dilute your point and may even backfire. Too little can make it difficult for your audience to understand or absorb your point, defeating your purpose either way. Think of it as surgery—you only want to take out what is essential and leave the rest.

Second, try out the depo lines on someone unfamiliar with the case, to be certain you have the impact you wish to have. What may be crystal clear to you may not be so clear to an outsider. And sometimes you may think there is more in a depo quote when you are reading it, but when you say it out loud you realize it does not have the effect you had envisioned, or you may stumble on a word out loud that you never would have known if you just read it to yourself.

Third, be *ethical* in how you select the lines you want to use to make a specific point, whether in court or out. Taking any type of testimony out of context to serve your own purpose not only violates legal ethics rules but also is the equivalent of yellow journalism. And it will usually bite you in the rear end eventually. There is no humiliation quite as acute as being called out on your misuse of a deposition quote. If you've ever seen a judge do this, you'll know what I'm talking about.

I've seen attorneys try to pull it off both in legal briefs and in oral/ motion arguments, and I've watched judges call attorneys on the carpet for it. It is never pretty. Once, I watched a judge sanction an attorney, her client, and her entire law firm—requiring every attorney in the firm to take ethics courses—all for taking testimony out of context. *Don't even think about it.*

Statutes

Quoting the law is usually only required or effective in a presentation in court or a legal education situation; the same rules regarding cases and deposition/hearing testimony apply to citing or quoting statutes. It can be used effectively, but my best advice is to use it sparingly and only to drive home a point, to set up an argument, in court, or to teach new law or a set of skills. It's a rare occasion when you see a member of your audience sit up straight in his or her seat to listen intently to an attorney reading a statute.

Opinions

There are court opinions, expert opinions, lay opinions, and my cousin Bobby's opinions. All are useful depending upon the context. For legal opinions, see my discussion under "Cases" above. For the remaining types of opinions, the same rules apply that I detailed in the "Deposition, Hearing, or Other Testimony" section earlier. As far as my cousin Bobby's opinions go, well, I don't know how helpful they will be, but usually they're pretty funny.

You need to use opinions strategically, usually as persuasive (or sometimes just funny) support for your point. However, be careful of using opinions too often.

Summing Up Step 2
I know this is a lot of information about the supporting materials for your speech, but the subject is worth this special attention. Giving yourself the best elements to work with and then using them to the best advantage is one of the easiest ways to ensure a successful presentation, yet speakers routinely underestimate the importance of this stage in the process. Now that we've given the research and gathering step the spotlight, we're ready to move on to organizing what you've pulled together.

Remember what I said at the beginning of the section on researching and gathering your support materials. I'm listing that as Step 2 and the next one as Step 3. But some people prefer to reverse the order. Once you read the next sections, you'll be able to find your own comfort zone and order to suit yourself.

Step 3: Decide Upon Your Three Main Points (and Use the Rule of Three)

Easy rule coming up, but one I can't overemphasize: *The easiest way for an audience to follow a presentation is if you organize it around three main points, topics, or concepts.*

People tend to remember groups of odd numbers: 3, 5, 7, 11. There is something about the rhythm associated with number sequences like this—phone numbers, Social Security numbers, zip codes—that make them easy to understand. To streamline your presentation and ensure that your major points are not lost, narrow your overall theme down to three main points.

To make your presentation clear and help your audience absorb your message, you want to assist them by categorizing and condensing your main ideas. And the easiest number of items for an audience to listen to is three, thus the "Rule of Three."

For example, if you were going to talk about driver safety, your major categories could be: Drive Defensively, Don't Be Distracted, and Arrive Alive. Once you have defined your three main points, you can offer them to the audience, explain that you're going to take them through each step one-by-one, and maybe even give them a mnemonic device to remember the steps.

My public speaking seminar presentations always have three main points: Audience, Message, Image. AMI™—remember? I use these three main points whether I am giving a one-hour keynote or a three-hour basic training seminar, or even a two-day in-depth seminar and coaching program. These three points are repeated many times during my presentation and, inevitably, when I reach the end of any presentation, each and every audience member can quote back to me my three main points and why they matter.

Make this your goal. Your audience should be able to tell you your three main points when you're through. If they can't, it means your message got lost in the details. Avoid the temptation to load down your message with lots of main points, like a Top 10 or Top 20 list. Simply put, keep it focused: Distill your information, find the themes, and turn those themes into your three main points.

Tip for Impromptu Presentations:

If you are surprised, or surprise yourself, and have to do an impromptu presentation, quickly write down three main points or ideas that you want to address. Do it on a napkin, a sheet of paper, your palm, whatever it takes. Then when you are speaking, make sure to glance down to those points to keep you on topic and on track. It's the best way to keep you organized and focused when doing an impromptu presentation.

Step 4: Choose How You Organize Your Points

Simply put, there are many ways to organize thoughts, ideas, and themes. Pick an organizational pattern that is right for your presentation. Here are four common options:

Sequential/Chronological

Does your presentation move through a series of points that can be organized in a sequential or chronological pattern? If so, do not attempt to jump around and explain your points nonsequentially or you will lose your audience. If the points you wish to make or the stories you have to relate occurred one at a time, stick to the chronology. Your audience will follow right along with you.

For example, when you read that two-page instruction manual that comes with your new electronic device, it always goes through each step in the right sequential order. Some topics just require this form of organization to be understood: What happened first? What happened second? Then what happened? How does it end?

Sometimes you can start with the end and work your way back, but you definitely can't skip around if a topic really needs a sequential presentation.

Think of it this way. Are you telling a story? Does it work to start the story in the middle, jump a bit to the beginning, then the end, then back to the middle? Nope. So evaluate what you have to communicate closely to see if any of it needs to be presented in a specific sequential order to ensure your audience understands it.

Categorical/Topical

As with the Audience, Message, Image example I cited above, some points are most easily organized by category or topic. When you have a lot of information you want to present, figure out the three categories or themes under which the information will fit and go with that. My example above, about AMI™, is a classic categorical approach.

When using a categorical approach, put your most important point first, your second most important point last, and then sandwich the other point in the middle. That way you're taking advantage of the Primacy/Recency theory, which holds that people best remember the first thing and the last thing they hear. However, that rule does not apply in an oral argument, where your points should be made in order of importance. See Chapter Eleven for more on this.

Problem–Solution

This is a simple way to both organize and present a speech cleanly and with little digression: Set up a problem and then offer a solution (or several solutions) to that problem.

Be sure that the problem is one common to most members of the audience (the more relevant you can be, the better) and try to offer novel or clever solutions rather than merely obvious ones. Within the problem–solution framework, you might discuss the causes and impacts of problems (such as gambling compulsions or addictions), review past or outmoded solutions that have failed, and, finally, provide a new or time-tested solution that is most likely to work.

Compare and Contrast

When making comparisons, be sure the comparisons are valid. Apples are not oranges. Don't make the mistake of mixing up the two. If you want to compare raising a child to raising a domestic animal, you run the risk of alienating the parents in the room. (Or the pet owners, for that matter.) But if you hit upon a comparison that works, by all means use it. The same rule applies to contrasts. Baseball is similar to football in that both are sports, both use a ball, and both employ a points system. In that way, you can compare the two. But there are also many ways you can contrast them and examine the differences. (George Carlin did this famously and to great effect.[2]) Using comparisons and contrasting examples is a wonderful way to hammer home your three main points.

Step 5: Create Your Outlines. Yes, Outlines.

Creating an outline can help you in several ways, but perhaps the most important of them is this: When you are finished with your outline, it should be all you need to hold in your hand, or place on the lectern, in order for you to deliver a presentation. A truly well-organized outline will allow you to sail through your presentation without a hitch.

The trick to creating an effective outline is to develop one that has just the *exact* amount of information you need—no more, no less. Put too much verbiage in your outline and you risk writing something you have to read verbatim, right off the page. Put too little on the page and you're likely to forget some important point that you meant to make.

So how do you manage this?

Be economical, but not stingy. Write the first take of your outline in full sentences.

When creating your outline, remember the acronym PEP[3]: Point, Explanation/Example, Point. Use this format throughout your presentation for optimum effect and to help your audience understand and remember what you are discussing.

PEP is exactly what it sounds like. You make your point, then you tell a story, an anecdote, an example or explanation, and you finish by reiterating your point. For example, when I teach public speaking I talk about making sure your humor isn't offensive, then I give the example of a former city councilman's inappropriate joke as an example (I'll get to it in Chapter Four), then I reiterate the point that you have to make sure any humor you use isn't offensive.

---

[2] In case you aren't familiar with this bit, you can find it many places on the net. Here is one transcript: http://www.baseball-almanac.com/humor7.shtml.

[3] The acronym PEP is not my own creation—it is one of the most effective speaking techniques I learned, way back in graduate school.

Once you have created your first outline, practice it. This cannot be emphasized enough. Each time you run through the presentation, you will make changes to your outline. You will reduce it, condense it, clarify it—in the end, you will have the kind of succinct outline that you know well enough to refer to only as needed.

You'll basically go from what we call a Full-Sentence outline to a Key-Word outline. Using this process is the essence of creating an extemporaneous speech.

When you reduce your Full-Sentence outline to key words and phrases, you'll want to keep the important information that you won't always be able to remember, such as quotes, story references, cites, and statistics.

This is why I say in the header to *create* your *outlines*—plural. You begin with one, but you will create at least two or three by the time you have finished practicing, editing, and practicing and editing some more.

Creating outlines is priceless when it comes to presenting. The more you do it, the more likely you are to succeed as a speaker.

Example:

When I created my three-hour Presentation Skills for Attorneys speech, the first outline was sixty-two pages long. I practiced it about four times and got it down to about thirty pages.

Since then I have worked it and reworked it so many times that it now varies between one page and twenty-one pages, roughly. The length of the outline depends upon the length of time I have to speak.

The other reason you practice it out loud and rework your outline, reducing it to a Key-Word outline, is to ensure your presentation stays on time. You won't know if your presentation is the right length time-wise, unless you practice it out loud. In fact, you are likely to find that the first time you practice it, you take much longer than the actual amount of time you have to present.

On the other hand, if you do not practice out loud, with your outline by your side, you will run into enormous trouble when the time comes to actually deliver your presentation. You will hem and haw, pause awkwardly, take too much time, or go off on too many tangents. There is only one way to avoid these traps: PRACTICE.

Reviewing the Five Steps to Build Your Message

As described above, there are five steps to creating your presentation. To review, they are:

1. Create a thesis statement.
2. Research and gather supporting materials.
3. Consolidate your *three* main points (remember the Rule of Three).
4. Choose how you organize your points.
5. Create your outline.

And remember, Steps 2 and 3 can be interchanged—you can do either first, just be sure to do both, especially #3.

Once you feel that you've arrived at a final Key-Word outline, make sure you hit your mark. Go back to the thesis statement you wrote down in Step 1 and see if your presentation outline accomplishes the goal stated in the thesis. If not, go back to Step 3 and rework from there.

I've worked with a lot of speakers over the years who end up with too much in their presentations—sometimes after we look at the goal of the presentation, half of what was included gets taken out for another day. That's the best way to evaluate your presentation: Review the outline and make sure it achieves your goal without being led astray with too many diversions.

Follow these basic steps and you'll find yourself crafting more memorable, and comprehensible, presentations.

And make sure you give yourself enough time to do it all. A lot of people, especially those who fear speaking, wait until the last minute before creating their presentation. As you can see from the steps I have listed, waiting until the last minute doesn't give you enough time to do it right, much less to do it well.

Do yourself—and your audience—a favor: Leave enough time to prepare well. You'll be happier with yourself and your presentation if you do.

CHAPTER FOUR

How You Start, Finish, and Move

In Chapter Three, I discussed the basic steps to creating a memorable message. Now I'm going to focus on what happens in the first few minutes and the last few minutes of your presentation, and how you get from Point A to Point B in all the time in between. But let's start at the very beginning: the introductory portion of your speech.

Why Does Your Introduction Matter?

Introductions serve a vital purpose. By "introduction," I don't mean how someone introduces you to the audience. Instead, I'm talking about the first part of your speech, where you introduce the subject you will be addressing. How you choose to start your speech is, in fact, one of the most important parts of your presentation. Why is that?

Simple. Your introduction is where you establish your own credibility and communicate your ethos. This is your opportunity to connect with the audience and establish a rapport. It is the moment where you can grab their attention and pique their curiosity and interest.

In these moments, you also provide a road map of the presentation—a preview, where you "tell them what you're going to tell them."

When I coach clients and speak at seminars, one of my jobs is to help people reframe their thinking about presentations. Most people who aren't trained in public speaking skills focus the bulk of their time on creating and honing the body of their presentation, and they give their introductions and conclusions short shrift.

This is a bad idea.

Think of your introduction as a first date. You might be able to rescue yourself from a bad beginning, but why start out at a disadvantage if you can help it? Similarly, when delivering a presentation, you only have a few moments to make that all-important first impression. If you don't pay strict attention to crafting an effective introduction, you may lose your audience before you even get to the core of your speech.

Simply put, it is *impossible* to establish your credibility, connect with your audience, grab their attention, and pique their curiosity if you don't carefully think about how you want to start off to accomplish these goals. So good introductions are critical to the success of your presentation.

Now that you know that introductions actually serve a purpose, let's look at what goes in them and how to deliver them.

What Should Go into Your Introduction?

Your Attention-Getter

The most effective introductions start with a compelling story, a thoughtful quote, or a startling statement to grab the audience's attention. Some people use rhetorical questions (or real questions) effectively. A staccato list of shocking statistics can also work. An anecdote and humor can start a speech off right, if done appropriately and well (i.e., if it is not an offensive or clichéd joke with no relevance to your topic).

I've described each of these tools as well as others and illustrated how they work below. It is important for you to choose which of them best suits *your* introduction and then also think about how to employ these methods at the right time throughout your speech.

Stories, Examples, and Anecdotes

If you decide to start with a story, you will, naturally, want to present something that is compelling and interesting, something that will tug on your audience's emotions. Keep your story brief and to the point; don't ramble on forever or digress into minute details. Keep it relevant. Make sure that the subject matter of the story is directly related to your speech and the overall message you want to communicate. It can have a moral, if you like, or it can just be a story that illustrates an issue, problem, challenge, or success related to the message in your presentation.

The key to telling a story is keep it simple and use your voice and body language to tell it well (see Chapter Seven, "Pitch-Perfect Delivery," for tips on that). Provide just enough detail to keep your listeners interested without overwhelming them or losing them.

Your guiding mantra when employing a story in your introduction should be **Grab their attention; don't put them to sleep.**

So how do you choose an appropriate story to begin your presentation? Sometimes, the answer presents itself in the topic of your speech. For example, if you're talking about workplace safety, you might want to begin with a story of an individual or a company that chose to take a shortcut or to overlook a safety feature, which choice caused someone to be injured.

If your tale is going to be a cautionary one, however, it is important that the lesson be memorable, not mundane. Relating a story about a store manager whose oversight resulted in a customer's minor injury is hardly earth-shattering. On the other hand, telling a story about an engineer who missed a safety check and caused a missile explosion is bound to grab some interest. You don't have to shoot for the "if it bleeds, it leads" scenario, but you don't want your story to fall flat either. Too often, I've heard speakers who attempt to shock and awe their audiences with a final line of their speech (" . . . and it turned out that *the vending machine was empty the whole time*") only to have the audience yawn when they should have been gasping.

Generally speaking, you want to tell a story about something that actually happened (audiences can sense when you're snowing them)—if you were personally involved or witnessed the occurrence, all the better.

Finally, when you start to relate your story, it is important that you do everything you can to conjure the "magic of the moment." You want your story to be suspenseful or interesting, so telling it as if you've said it a hundred times before isn't going to cut it. You have to lead up to the surprising moments as if you didn't know they were coming. You have to be shocked at whatever is shocking. You need to empathize with anyone who is hurt or wronged in the course of your story. Become emotionally involved in the story you're telling, and the audience will be with you all the way.

And vary your vocals! Stories are boring if told in monotone, too quickly, or too slowly. See "Vary Your Vocals" in Chapter Seven, "Pitch-Perfect Delivery," to learn how to deliver a story with impact.

Shocking Statistics

Shocking statistics wake people up and grab their attention in a way that few other speaking tools do. Shocking statistics make people think. When used properly, they make people feel. Use shocking statistics for effect and deliver them with impact (see "Delivering Your Introduction" below and "Pitch-Perfect Delivery" in Chapter Seven).

Why are statistics so effective? Because people *believe* in them. Statistics are used in everyday life to such a degree—for elections, sports, schooling, you name it—that we have come to trust in the use of statistics to explain almost anything.

Did you know that 95 percent of Americans never question statistics at all? It's true! (Actually, it isn't true. I made it up. But you believed it for a second there, didn't you? Because I presented it *as a statistic.* See the way that works?)

A word of caution, however: use statistics sparingly, especially in your introduction. You can get away with one to three statistics in your introduction—*if* they are truly revelatory and will move people—but no more than three. If you overuse this technique, you will end up boring your audience or confusing them. The reason for this is because it is hard to track the oral recitation of a lot of statistics. People will tune you out quickly. (And no, that doesn't mean you can put a bunch of statistics up on a PowerPoint slide in order to use more than three. It means don't use more than three. Period.)

Don't risk losing your audience by citing too many statistics in your introduction. Like anything else that is enjoyable (coffee, ice cream, relatives), there can sometimes be too much of a good thing. So learn how to limit yourself.

Also, when possible, give a *source* for your statistics to add to the credibility and weight of your statement. If your statistics are from a source known for its accuracy and honesty (especially if the source is close to the heart of your listeners), you add credibility to yourself in the process of quoting that source.

This can be a double-edged sword, of course. Quoting a source that your audience may not trust (e.g., citing a Fox News statistic at the Democratic National Convention) might not be the best choice for you to make your point. Make sure your statistics are credible and accurate and have the proof to back yourself up if challenged.

Another thing you can do with statistics is to use a rapid-fire approach technique to deliver them, whether in your introduction or in your speech. Very quickly state two or three critical statistics. Boom, boom, boom. Then pause for effect, make eye contact, and slowly restate the most important or most shocking statistic.

This technique can be used in multiple settings, in or out of court. Let me give you one such scenario:

Picture yourself speaking at a seminar. You are sitting at a panel table and instead of kicking off your talk with name, rank, and serial number (meaning name, title, and law firm), you stand up, walk around the table, look your audience members in the eye, and rattle off two to three statistics about how frequently attorneys fail their clients by doing x, y, and z and how much that costs the attorney or clients, or the legal system, when the failure occurs.

Now *that* would grab your audience's attention. Moreover, it would set you apart from the rest of the speakers on your panel. (Warning: They might get jealous; you can send them a copy of my book or DVD if they do.)

Another example: Picture yourself having to do a presentation on the subject of sexual harassment.

You start off with:

"According to recent polls, more than 50 percent of women have experienced unwanted and inappropriate advances from male colleagues at work—a quarter of these victims said the male colleagues who harassed them had power over their careers.

And according to an Equal Employment Opportunity Commission study done in 2016, 75 percent of women harassed at work never bother to report it out of fear of retaliation or not being believed. 75 percent of women who are harassed at work do not report it. 75 percent!

We can hope, however, that that number will change. In response to a rapidly growing number of high-profile men accused of sexual harassment and assault in the workplace, the "me too" campaign on Twitter has put a spotlight on the problem at large. And the specific public allegations that helped launch the "me too" campaign have resulted in the immediate firing and resignations of the high-profile men accused of years of harassment.

It's time to take a closer look at the culture of sexual harassment in the workplace, why it is so discounted, and how the current spotlight on harassment can cause real change."

In this example, instead of starting off by introducing yourself and saying you'll be discussing the rise of sexual harassment in the workplace (both of which will make your audience's eyes glaze over), you chose to first grab their attention and give them a tangible, real reason to listen to you.

Once you've done that, you're off and running.

Startling Statements

Startling statements work much the same way as shocking statistics, they just don't include statistics. Again, if you're going to try to be shocking, don't over- or undersell your statement. Remember to say something that is *actually* shocking but, at the same time, not *so* shocking so as to offend the listeners. This is a delicate balance, of course, and there are inherent risks to trying to shock your crowd right off the bat. But there are also great rewards, not the least of which is grabbing their full attention with the first words out of your mouth.

Thoughtful Quotes

Starting off with a citation or a quote happens to be my favorite speaking technique, mainly because I am a quote geek. Quotes are an extremely effective means of grabbing an audience's attention, and the beauty of quotes is that you don't have to think up the words yourself.

To employ this technique, you must spend some time finding a quote that relates to your topic and will make your audience think, or laugh, or both. Research your theme or topic, and search for relevant quotes online or in one of the many quote-compilation books. Once you have found one that suits you perfectly, be sure to copy it down *exactly as written* and be sure that the quote is accurate.

I cannot emphasize this point enough. Too often these days, quotes are misattributed and lines are taken out of context. My favorite satirical example:

> "The thing about quotes on the internet is that you cannot confirm their validity."
>
> *—Abraham Lincoln*

However, once you have your quote and have sourced it properly, it can prove to be the best way to launch you into your speech.

Start off right away with your quote. And when I say, "right away," I mean it. Don't begin with your name, or by thanking the committee for inviting you to speak, or by mentioning how honored you are to be there. All those things may be true, but none of them will grab your audience's attention. Instead, start with the quote before you say *anything* else. Then, once you've served it up, tie the quote to your presentation by providing a few comments on it as it relates to your key message.

If you need to introduce yourself, or do some housekeeping—like asking people to turn their cell phones to vibrate—do it *after* your attention-getter and before your preview (I'll get to your preview in a minute).

If you've chosen wisely, you'll have both the audience's respect and their attention.

If you can, however, avoid waxing poetic about how meaningful the quote is to you personally. It never pays to guild the lily too much. Let the quote be the effective tool that it can be and then move on.

Asking Questions to Identify with the Audience

Some speakers begin their presentations by asking the audience questions related to the audience, or to the audience's perception of relevant topics. One advantage of starting in this way is to immediately get your audience participating in the presentation and interacting with you. In addition, you can learn more about your audience on a mass level if you invite them to be active participants from the beginning.

The disadvantage of employing this technique is that if used incorrectly, you can very easily start off on the wrong foot or take up too much time at the beginning of your presentation. If you try to engage the audience and find them to be completely unresponsive, you have the potential to look foolish or somehow not in control. As I've already mentioned, introductions should be brief, to the point, and engaging.

If you would like to use this technique and reach out to your audience from the beginning, there are three ways you can ensure it goes well.

1. **Keep it short**—Don't ask more than two or three questions. There is a fine line between feeling engaged as an audience and feeling interrogated. And the last thing you want to do is to annoy your audience in the first minute of your speech. They, like you, want you to keep things moving and get to the point. It's also annoying if you spend the first ten minutes of your forty-minute speech asking questions of the audience.
2. **Don't overanalyze**—Once you get your audience talking, don't spend time analyzing the audience's response. Instead, briefly comment on how they answer your questions, if warranted, and then move on. A lot of speakers can get bogged down or sidetracked by a particular answer or response. Guard against this whenever possible.
3. **Give instructions**—Remember to tell your audience how they should respond when you ask a question (i.e., "just shout out your answer" or "raise your hand if . . . ") Otherwise, the audience won't really know how they are supposed to respond and in some cases *if* they are supposed to respond (if it sounds like a rhetorical question). You don't want your first interaction with them to be an awkward pause.

If you haven't had time to interact with your audience one-on-one prior to your speech, as described in Chapter One of this book, these first few moments give you a chance to check in with them and find out a little bit more about them with a question. For example, you could say, "Raise your hand if you've been practicing law more than five years," or "Raise your hand if you've ever filed an appeal." Their responses to these questions will allow you to get the information you need to adjust your presentation according to your audience's answers. Sometimes the responses will surprise you and allow you to either emphasize or deemphasize certain aspects of your speech. For example, if you discover that no one in your audience has filed an appeal, you'll want to be sure to spend a little extra time explaining the process, if that is what they need to understand the rest of your presentation.

Example:

When a colleague of mine was discussing this topic, she told me that she uses this method a lot—especially to determine how many lawyers, accountants, or life insurance professionals are in the audience when she is on an estate planning panel.

The best time she used it, she said, was at a national meeting of Tax Accountant members of the AICPA (Association of International Certified Professional Accountants). It was a huge audience, and she was using an interactive PowerPoint Q & A application that allowed audience members to respond directly to the question. The audience either had clickers or used their cell phones to answer the question she posted.

The question? How many of you know a married same-sex couple? The answer? three percent. It was a dramatic way to make a point and interact with the audience.

Of course, the question-and-answer technique is one that you can use throughout your presentation to ensure you are meeting the needs of your audience and not speaking under or over their heads—as well as keeping them engaged. (It never hurts to check in with an "Are there any questions about that?" at certain points during your presentation, if you want to get a sense of how they are following along.)

And if you *did* find the time to interact with the audience one-on-one before the presentation, your introduction is an opportunity to connect more directly with them by mentioning someone by name in relation to the topic or your pre-speech discussion. People like to be recognized and remembered. They especially like to be praised in front of their peers. There is a concept in both psychology and marketing called "affinity." It explains how people tend to like people who appear to like them. Dale Carnegie was a big proponent of this line of thinking. Show an interest in another person or find a connection with them and more likely than not they will reciprocate.

You can use this technique to create a closer connection with your audience by mentioning someone in the room by name—always in a positive manner—and by incorporating something you discussed before the program into your presentation (this is *not*, needless to say, the time to use sarcasm). When you do this, you create the impression that you know and like that person, and this helps to create a positive feeling among audience members.

Why does this occur? In a presentation setting, there is the "us"—the audience—and the "them"—the speaker(s). As a speaker, you want to always try to breach the "us-them" dynamic. By using this engagement technique, you help to bridge that gap. Or as I sometimes say, you break down the audience-speaker barrier.

Referring to the Event
Another way to immediately engage your audience is by tying your talk into the overall event or something that has occurred since you all arrived at the venue. This is most applicable when you're speaking at a multiday conference, but the technique can also be applied in court or at various business settings.

If you have a funny story about something that occurred at the event, it can be a nice, light way to start off and grab everyone's attention (everyone wants to hear about what is going on around them), and it helps you tie yourself to your audience and your surroundings. If you have a serious story, it can be a dramatic way to kick off a presentation as long as you are careful not to touch on raw nerves.

This last method can be risky, as your story will not often be time-tested; but if pulled off with the right degree of dramatic flair, it can be just the trick to get the crowd on your side from the start.

Rhetorical Questions
What is a good example of a rhetorical question?

The difference between a rhetorical question and a real question is that with the former, you do not expect an answer, and with the latter, you do. The advantage of using a rhetorical question as your attention-getter is that the best rhetorical questions are designed to make your audience think and, therefore, engage their attention.

The difficulty is in picking the right rhetorical question—something that has drama or impact—and in delivering the question with the right emphasis to bring out the drama you intend. Here are some tips on how to make your rhetorical question more effective:

- Make sure you make eye contact and pause after the question, but only briefly. If you pause for too long, your audience will begin to get uncomfortable and wonder if you actually wanted an answer to the question, or worse, they will try to answer it and effectively ruin the impact of the question. If this happens, you can make a self-deprecating joke and use the laugh as the attention-getter/icebreaker instead.
- Answer the rhetorical question as soon as you can. You'd be surprised how many speakers employ rhetorical questions and then neglect to answer them. It is, as you can imagine, extremely annoying.
- Do not overuse this technique. Asking a rhetorical question as an introduction to each new point you want to make in your presentation is a common trap that speakers blunder into. Don't let it happen to you. If you find that your presentation has a number of these types of questions, try to whittle them down to one or two at the most if you can.

Generally speaking, rhetorical questions can be a quick way to grab your audience's attention, but, like almost every other introductory device, they have their share of pitfalls.

Suspense

I once attended a presentation where the speaker began his presentation with a very moving story. He told it well, using pauses, repetition, and vocal variety to grab and hold our attention and create suspense. And getting our attention was not an easy task. This particular audience was full of members of a local chapter of the National Speakers Association—a *professional public speaker association*—and we were all busy chatting with each other and catching up when his presentation began.

But grab our attention he did—and more. When he got to the climax of the story, he had us all on the edge of our chairs waiting to hear what happened next. Just as it seemed he was going to get to the big finish, he surprised us all by moving directly into his main presentation instead of finishing the story.

You could hear a collective groan from the audience—we wanted to know how the story ended! But he had us hook, line, and sinker. For the next 45 minutes or so we were captivated by his presentation, and when his speech was finally drawing to a close, he returned to his story and finished it for us. It was an emotional, powerful story, and you could look around the room and see the impact it had on the audience. Even more importantly, the story he told had a direct correlation to the message he was communicating to us that day, which made the emotional punch of his presentation that much more effective.

Three important keys to using suspense, which is *very* effective:

1. Have a moving, good story to tell that builds to a climax and leaves the audience desperately wanting to hear the end.
2. Be a good storyteller; work on your vocals, your nonverbal cues, your presence, and your body movement to help you tell the story well and with impact.
3. Make sure the story has some point, real-world application, or cogent message that relates to the purpose of your speech and helps you communicate and reinforce that purpose.

Once you've got something like that to present, you've won the war before the battle has even begun.

A Deposition Quote

This idea sort of speaks for itself. A great line from a deposition (when speaking about law-related topics) can be as attention-getting as a great quote. In this case, you might not want to give an actual attribution (for the sake of propriety) to the case you were working on, but lawyers love to hear stories about Adventures in Litigation, so give them a treat if you can.

Humor

My cousin Bobby—now, he could tell a joke. I envied him. Me, not so much. I can't always remember the punch line, which, you might not be surprised to hear, is a joke-killer. So, in my presentations, I don't start with a joke.

If *you* can tell a joke, however, it can be a good way to begin your speech or, more accurately, a way to break the ice with your audience. But joke-telling (like so many other techniques) is inherently risky, and there are some basic rules by which you need to abide.

Rule number one: Tell your joke well and remember the punch line! (Seems obvious, but it needs to be said.)

Rule number two: Don't tell a joke that is offensive in any manner whatsoever. I addressed this at the research/development stage in Chapter Two, but it's worth repeating. It's important enough that you have to actually run your joke by people to find out if it is offensive—preferably people who are not dependent upon you for either food or money. Why must you do this? Because

"Few people can see genius in someone who has offended them."

—*Robertson Davies*

What you think is offensive (or inoffensive) may or may not be perceived that way by someone else. And the worst way to begin a speech is to tick off your audience. Getting them back after that is virtually impossible. Not only that, but the folks you have offended are more likely to talk about that than anything else you said.

I thought I'd be pretty safe with 800-pound gorilla jokes. But as bad luck would have it, there was one in the audience.

Let me give you an example. In 2007 or 2008, I was with several of my colleagues, coaching a Los Angeles City Council person who will remain unnamed. I was coaching him, and he was doing an impromptu speech about how great a new shopping center would be for the community in his district. As he was describing the benefits of the very upscale, very expensive shopping center, he decided to tell a joke: "And the best thing about this shopping center is the fabulous new Neiman Marcus. Why? Because all the women out there can go out and spend their husbands' money."

Oh yeah.

It took half an hour to convince Mr. City Council person that the joke was not only bad, but also offensive, and I am still not sure I got through to him. At first, he felt that we were being too politically correct. Let me assure you, this isn't about being politically correct; it is about meeting the needs of your audience and not offending them. That's it.

Another time I was doing an in-house program at a mid-sized law firm in Northern California when this topic came up. In response, a senior partner raised his hand and asked, "But what if it's a really funny joke and you only offend 10 percent of your audience?" He was serious, and he got a great laugh out of the assembled participants, but I had an answer for him:

You don't want to offend anyone in your audience, not even a mere 10 percent, because as soon as you offend even a portion of your audience, they will begin to tune you out. Their body language shows it, and it becomes contagious. The people near them tend to notice as members of the audience disengage from a speaker, and pretty soon much of the group has withdrawn their attention and approval. And why would you want to alienate even one person in your audience after spending so much time preparing a great presentation?

The risk is not worth the perceived reward. So don't try it. If you tell a joke, make sure it's not offensive.

Here is the final rule with jokes: As I mentioned in Chapter Three, they work better during an introduction if the joke has some connection to your presentation topic or purpose. This means that your joke has to be relevant. Otherwise, it's just a joke.

So if you're going to be funny, be funny with a purpose.

Your Self-Introduction (If Necessary)

For the few times you may be forced to introduce yourself (in out-of-court settings), there are a few basic guidelines.

First, keep in mind that your self-introduction is *not* an attention-getter. So start with your attention-getter, *then* introduce yourself and make any housekeeping announcements (like reminding audience members to turn off their cell phones), and *then* go into your preview of your presentation. I discuss that below.

For your self-introduction, you'll want to just mention a few relevant points about your background that will help reinforce the credibility you began establishing with your attention-getter. Skip where you went to school unless it is somehow relevant to your audience (e.g., you are speaking at your alumni association). Also skip the nitty-gritty details like your massive publication list; your audience should have that information in the written biography you (hopefully) provided to the relevant person to include in the written materials.

So, to repeat, the order from the beginning is your attention-getter, your self-introduction, any housekeeping details, then the preview.

If you are wondering why you structure your introduction in this way, it is because the standard, overused, and entirely unimpressive method of beginning a presentation—*"Hi, I'm Faith Pincus, and I've been teaching public speaking for decades. I want to thank so-and-so for inviting me here today and I want to thank you for coming to listen to me today . . . "*—does nothing to grab your audience's attention, add to your credibility, or create a connection with your audience. It is boring and generic, which means that your first words to your audience are, in essence: *"I am uncreative and mediocre. Nice to meet you."* Stay away from it.

Your Preview

This is the "tell them what you're going to tell them" portion of the program. You want to clue your audience in on what you will be talking about the rest of the time they will be, hopefully, listening to you.

The basic rules on your preview: Keep it simple. Keep it direct. Keep it short. And above all, don't start delving into explanations or details about your three main points. I hear a lot of speakers who try to explain concepts in their introductions, right in the middle of their previews. This isn't the time to do that. Just give the audience a broad overview about what you will be addressing and maybe why it matters, and then move on.

Here's an example of the preview I use in my public speaking seminars:

> "We're going to discuss three things today: Audience, Message, and Image—AMI. These are the three most important things you need to know about public speaking.

You must know who your audience is, and you must cater your message to them.

You must craft a careful, interesting, and *organized* message.

And you *must* pay attention to, and develop, an interesting and *dynamic* image and delivery style.

Those are the keys to public speaking. Audience, Message, Image—just remember AMI. Those are three things you need to know to improve your public speaking in any setting. Whether you're before a judge or jury; speaking to a huge group at a public event; testifying to a city council on behalf of your real estate client; or reporting to your board of directors.

It doesn't matter what setting you're in, that's what you need to focus on.

So let's get started with your Audience . . . ."

I keep it simple, I use repetition for impact and to reinforce the message, I mention why it matters (that the three main ideas apply in most public speaking settings), and I employ an acronym—AMI™—to make it easy to remember.

Keeping your introduction short means keeping it less than five minutes long. My introduction is less than five minutes in duration whether I am speaking for fifty minutes, ninety minutes, or three hours (or even all day). Focus on the purpose of your introduction—establishing your credibility, connecting with your audience, grabbing their attention, and giving them a preview of what is to come—and you'll be able to create a five-minute introduction

It may take you a little bit to hone the skill of creating a preview to the point where you can grab an audience right off the bat and hold their attention, but once you've gained that advantage, you're already miles ahead of the average public speaker.

Delivering a Successful Introduction

Quite simply, the most effective way to *deliver* your introduction is to make eye contact with your audience for the entire duration of your introduction. This is both the most terrifying and most thrilling part of a speech before a live audience. But before we get into that, let's talk about why eye contact is so important.

Remember the beginning of this chapter? The introduction helps you establish your credibility and it lets you connect with your audience.

You can do neither of these things if you are reading off an outline and not looking your audience in the eyes.

Besides, if you don't know what your name is and what you're talking about without looking at your notes, you're going to have a hard time establishing your credibility or connecting with your audience, that's for sure.

The easiest way to ensure you can deliver your introduction while making eye contact is to rehearse it to the point that you have it basically memorized (and, of course, keep it short!). If your introduction is created as described above, it will be very brief—just long enough to accomplish your goals. As I mentioned earlier, my in-depth public speaking training presentation is more than three hours long. The introduction? Five minutes. Max. No more than that. And it is the same length, whether I am doing a fifty-minute keynote or a three-hour training speech.

Take a minute to reflect on the speeches you have heard, good and bad. Of the less-successful presentations, think about those you've heard where the speaker's introduction went on and on and on. When this happens, the audience usually starts wondering if the speaker will ever get to the point of the presentation and will begin to doubt that the speaker will have time to deal with all the points to be addressed. "Will the speaker keep droning on like this? Will the speaker run long and take the next speaker's time or, worse, will this mean less time for lunch? What good books have I read lately? What's that going on outside the window?" Whatever it is, it's bound to be more interesting than this speech.

You don't want to be that speaker.

You need to *accomplish your purpose.* You need to connect with your audience, establish your credibility, give your three main points, and grab people's attention. You can do that in five minutes. And you can—you must—practice this enough that you know it by heart. I'm not talking about writing down every single word and then remembering exactly what you've written. That won't give you the best results, and it is bound to look inflexible and robotic. Give yourself just enough notes to execute the introduction the way you want it to come out. And then start doing it without looking at your notes. Don't be daunted by this challenge because, if you create a succinct introduction, it should only take a few minutes to have it memorized. Naturally, if your introduction is twenty minutes long, you're going to have a much harder time memorizing it.

So make eye contact and give them an introduction that you've memorized and rehearsed. Do this, and you will have accomplished the primary objectives of your introduction.

Catchy Conclusions

Like introductions, conclusions are usually overlooked yet are incredibly important to giving an effective presentation. People tend to remember the first and last thing they hear (see the Primacy/Recency Theory data at right).

In other words, just as you want to begin your speech with a bang, you want to end on a strong note as well.

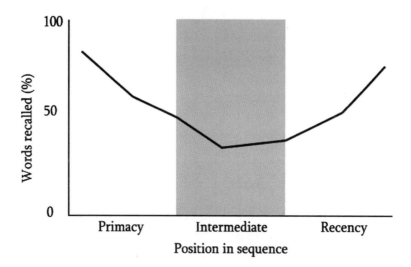

What's the Purpose?

Conclusions have several functions. The best of them are working on multiple levels.

First, conclusions exist to summarize your main points, reinforce your message, and help your audience remember your primary themes. This is where you want to drive home your main points one final time. It is the tried-and-true speaking tool called "tell them what you told them."

Conclusions are also an opportunity to reinforce your image. To end with impact. To leave your audience thinking.

If you have a call-to-action, this is where it goes. For in-court presentations, you ask the judge for what you want at both the beginning and the end of your presentation. Always. For out-of-court presentations, you don't always want to start with your "ask," because often you need to lay the foundation and persuade people before you ask for action. But you do want it at the end without question.

When I ran public affairs campaigns a long time ago, my boss would describe what we did—campaigns and speeches alike—as follows: **Educate, Motivate, Activate.**

Speeches that ask for something do this. If you are going to ask your audience to do something (or think about something or, even trickier, *change their minds* about something), the best place to give the "ask" is at the end, after you have educated and motivated them. In this way, you are far more likely to get a positive response. Why? Because you've given them a reason to want to do what it is you are asking them to do (or think about) *and*, hopefully, you've given them some form of motivation to actually do it. If you start with the call-to-action or "the ask" before you've given them any reason why they should respond, you will encounter more resistance.

Conclusions also allow you to wrap everything up neatly and provide closure. This isn't as obvious as it sounds. I have attended many presentations where the speaker just ends. The presentation stops suddenly, without the speaker taking the time to wrap things up. Even worse, I have heard speakers go completely off topic right at the conclusion and start discussing something entirely new. Forever and ever and ever. You can see the audience writhing in their seats when this happens. They thought they were free, but now they're trapped and they don't know when they're going to get released. It's worse than a bad horror movie. A proper conclusion helps your audience anticipate the end.

And, as mentioned at the beginning of this section, conclusions allow you, the speaker, to end on a positive, strong note. It is essential that you take advantage of this opportunity.

What Goes into a Strong Conclusion?

Your conclusion should be as simple as your introduction:

- Summarize your three main points.
- Make a reference to and/or utilize the attention-getting device you used in your introduction.
- And of course give your ask—if there is one.

One effective way to provide closure—with impact—is to somehow use or reference the attention-getting device you use to kick off your presentation. You may want to refer to the story you told the audience, or maybe you repeat one of the statistics you used. Retelling a joke won't work (another reason not to use a joke in an introduction), but you can incorporate the moral of the joke, as you would the moral of a fable, into the fabric and ending point of your message.

How you reference your attention-getting device depends upon the device used, but it is important to "work" it into your message and use it to drive home your theme. The best way to explain what I mean is by example.

Remember the attention-getter at the beginning of my presentation? I may or may not make reference to it again in the body of the speech. But then, at the end of my speech, I use that same quote, story, or statistic and *incorporate* it into my concluding points. I work the attention-getter into my theme to drive home my message; I don't just restate it.

Practice Tip:

How do I actually do that? Say my attention-getting quote in my introduction is this: "Someone once said the mind is a beautiful thing. The mind is a wonderful thing. The mind starts working the moment we are born. And it never stops working—until the moment we stand up to speak in public."[1]

When I am at the end of my presentation I will incorporate that quote like this: " . . . in conclusion, we talked about a lot of things today that will help you become a better public speaker. We talked about how you always have to remember AMI when creating, and delivering, your presentations. Audience, Message, and Image. You *must* find out who your audience is and meet their needs. You *must* craft a careful and *organized* message. And you *must* develop an interesting and dynamic delivery style—one that also works with your personality.

I'm going to end with the quote that I started with, which by now you already know inside and out: 'Someone once said that the mind is a beautiful thing. The mind is a wonderful thing. The mind starts working the moment we are born. And it never stops working—until the moment we stand up to speak in public.'

Today you've learned a lot about public speaking—you've learned some beginner tips and some advanced tips, and you've learned enough that the *next* time you get up to speak in public, your mind will *keep* working, and you'll do a wonderful job of it."

---

[1] The verbatim quote is by Judge George Jessel (1824–1883): "The human brain starts working the moment you are born and never stops until you stand up to speak in public." Because I draw it out and embellish it—a lot—for maximum impact, I do not quote him directly (as that would be misquoting him).

This speaking technique requires you to think about what you're going to say at the end of your presentation almost as much as you think about what you are going to say at the beginning. Furthermore, it requires you to create the body of your presentation *before* you create either your introduction or your conclusion. And it requires you to create your introduction before you create your conclusion.

You also want to keep your conclusion short, just like your introduction. Speakers who say "in conclusion" and then ramble on for fifteen to twenty minutes, drive their audiences nuts. When you start your conclusion with a transition that indicates you are ending your presentation ("In conclusion . . . "), you are making an implied promise to your audience that you are actually going to end your presentation. If you ramble on too long or start on a new topic, you have violated that implied promise. And then you run the risk of annoying your audience to the point of giving back some of the great impression you made early on in your presentation.

Making the Ending Count

We end the way we begin: with eye contact and a *memorized* final conclusion.

Why memorize it? Well, first, you can't exactly make eye contact with your audience if you are referring to your notes while attempting to conclude your presentation.

Second, as with your intro, if you don't know what it is you talked about and cannot summarize it without looking at your notes, you're in trouble. You don't have to memorize it word-for-word or line-by-line. All you need to do is practice it so much that you know exactly what you want to say and how you want to say it. Do that and you can easily sum things up at the end without looking at your notes.

Why use eye contact? Because without it, you cannot credibly reinforce your message, drive home your points, ask for something—*anything*—or end on a strong note. In the United States people trust people who look them in the eye. It is critical that you get your face out of your notes and make eye contact with your audience when you begin and when you conclude a presentation. (By the way, if you are in a different country or speaking to an audience from an unfamiliar culture, you must research the customs to ensure you do not make a *faux pas* here. Too much eye contact can come off as aggressive or immodest in some cultures.)

Effective Transitions

Transitions matter. Truly effective transitions help your audience follow you from one idea to the next, from one topic to the next. The good news is that transitions are easy. They just require a few cues to make sure your audience keeps up with you.

A common problem with public speakers occurs when they assume the audience knows where they are going to go before they get there. This is a dangerous assumption to make. Even a powerful speaker can derail his or her speech in a moment by suddenly jumping head first into a new topic without taking the time to bring the audience along for the ride.

To avoid this, take the necessary steps to let your audience know when one topic has been concluded and another topic has been introduced. You can be casual about it, using simple transitory words like "first," "second," "third," or "next." Or you can make it more formal (e.g., "Now I'd like to move on to a new topic … " or "I think we've sufficiently covered that. Let's take a look at this next.")

Easy transition words and phrases also include:

- Moving on
- The next issue
- The next argument
- The next …
- Now let's take a look at, or now let's think about, or now let's discuss.

Apart from these, there is another type of transition called "looking backwards and looking forwards." When you use that method, you refer to what you just spoke about and then mention what you are going to cover next. For example, "We just took a look at introductions; now let's talk about transitions," or "Now that we've looked at how you create your message, we are going to take a break and afterwards we'll start talking about effective delivery techniques."

Sometimes you will find yourself without a logical segue or neat transition. Maybe what you have to say next is a complete departure from your previous topic and you're worried that you could confuse your audience. You don't need to view this as a problem. Instead, try to turn it to your advantage by *acknowledging* the odd transition. You may even get a laugh. ("Okay, we've been talking about statistics for a while. Now I'd like to change things up a bit and chat about Dungeons and Dragons. Everybody saw that coming, right? Stay with me, people!")

The point about transitions is that speakers need to use them and use them often. Without transitions, you are asking your audience to drive from Los Angeles to New York without any road or street signs. Not a pretty picture.

CHAPTER FIVE

Rhetorically Speaking

Rhetorical techniques have been around since the days of the Ancient Greeks. If they were good enough for Aristotle and Socrates, they're good enough for you.

These techniques are persuasive tools that are useful in the same way as pausing and can have an *enormous* impact on your audience during a presentation. What's more, they're easy—anyone can learn them and use them. Let's start with the basics:

Similes and Metaphors

As you probably remember from elementary school, similes compare one thing to another by using the term "like" or "as." Metaphors compare one thing to another as well but without the "like" or "as." You don't need to recall the difference as long as you use both.

Almost every cliché you've ever heard is either a simile or a metaphor. A few examples:

- **Similes**—"Tough as leather." "Clear as a bell." "Hard as nails." "Dry as a bone." "Old as the hills." That sort of thing.
- **Metaphors**—"Judges are bilingual; they speak Plaintiff and Defendant." "He has a heart of gold." "Too much of the world is run on the theory that you don't need road manners if you are a five-ton truck." Quotes that are metaphors (many good ones are):
  - "Get someone else to blow your horn and the sound will carry twice as far." (Often attributed to Will Rogers.)
  - "Each day is a scroll: Do not write anything upon it that you do not want remembered." (B. ibn Pachav, eleventh century)

Let's take a look at a famous example from a movie that uses both similes and metaphors:

> And he was eighteen when we met, and I was Queen of France. He came down from the north to Paris with a mind like Aristotle's and a form like mortal sin. We shattered the commandments on the spot.—Katherine Hepburn, *The Lion in Winter.*

The middle sentence, as you can see, contains two similes. The last sentence contains the metaphor. And it sounds a lot better than, "When he got here I thought he was pretty smart and really cute and, well, we did a lot of things that maybe we weren't supposed to do back behind the tent."

Find strategic moments in your speech to employ both similes and metaphors when you need a rhetorical flourish to make a point.

Analogies

Analogies are lengthy metaphors or long similes that draw out the comparison in a way in which people can relate to most directly. One of my favorite examples comes from the singer Bono of the band U2 delivering the 2004 Commencement Address at the University of Pennsylvania:

> I don't think there's anything certainly more unseemly than the sight of a rock star in academic robes . . . . It's a bit like when people put their King Charles spaniels in little tartan sweats and hats . . . . It's not natural . . . and it doesn't make the dog any smarter.

Everyone nods and laughs when I play this quote in a public speaking skills seminar. The irony is not lost on anyone.

And here's one from George Bernard Shaw: "I learned long ago, never to wrestle with a pig. You get dirty, and besides, the pig likes it."

Rhetorical Questions

The rhetorical question is the question that does not require an answer. When delivered properly, it is clear that the answer is obvious. Some famous examples:

> "Sir, at long last, have you left no sense of decency?"—Joseph Welch, The Army-McCarthy Hearings

"Can anyone look at our reduced standing in the world today and say, 'Let's have four more years of this'?"—Ronald Reagan (This one has been used as both a rhetorical question and as a call and response question, to work up an audience.)

The danger in trying out a rhetorical question is if it backfires. As I mentioned earlier, you don't want to find yourself in the situation where your audience actually answers you back. So be sure to move on quickly to your next point before giving them a chance to do so.

I appreciate the spirited response. But actually, I meant "So what do we think?" to be more of a rhetorical question.

Alliteration

Alliteration is the first consonant or sound of a word, repeated in two or more consecutive words, across a phrase, clause or sentence.

Famous examples:

- "Reduce, Reuse, Recycle." (U.S. Environmental Protection Agency)
- "Sweet smell of success."
- "Isn't that what being an international man of mystery is all about?" (Mike Myers as Austin Powers)

Alliteration can be found in names (Marilyn Monroe, Barry Bonds, Katie Couric), in products (Coca-Cola, PayPal), and in pop culture ("Rudolph the Red-Nosed Reindeer"). These days you even find it at the airport ("When You See Something, Say Something"). The repetition of the sound forces you to remember it.

And while we're on the subject . . .

Repetition

Repetition is a powerful way to drive home a point. But, keep in mind, there is a distinct difference between bad repetition and good repetition.

Bad repetition is making a point that you've already made over and over again. If you do this, you risk alienating your audience because, in essence, you're treating them like idiots. (That redundancy comes across as, "You might not have gotten it the first time, so let me say it three more times to make sure you do.") And sometimes it's just plain boring.

Good repetition is a means of sending home an important point by saying something again for emphasis and impact, while still respecting your audience's collective intelligence.

One of the best examples of the successful use of repetition is Martin Luther King Jr.'s "I Have A Dream" speech. Dr. King uses a multitude of beautiful rhetorical techniques in that speech, but what is most remembered is his use of "I have a dream." That speech was 21 paragraphs long. Dr. King didn't start saying "I have a dream" until the sixteenth paragraph. Then he said it seven times.

And today, every single time I do a public speaking training program, every single person in that audience knows who said "I have a dream", what the phrase means, when it was said (if not the exact year), and usually where it was said. Some heard it live on the radio, and there have been two times that someone in my audience said they saw Dr. King deliver it live.

But even the youngest generations know what the phrase means. Why? Because of its lasting power. Why is it powerful enough to have lasted this long? That legacy is at least partly due to a masterful use of rhetorical dynamics—because of the use of repetition to drive home his significant message. This phrase and several others (like "Let Freedom Ring") are examples of how to use repetition for effect.

You might be surprised to learn that there are many different types of repetition. Let's review a few (which can be found on AmericanRhetoric .com):

- **Epistrophe**—An epistrophe is a word or phrase repeated at the end of a sentence, phrase, or clause. Abraham Lincoln used this technique in the Gettysburg Address when he promised " . . . that government of the people, by the people and for the people shall not perish from the earth."
  - George C. Scott, in the film *Patton*, had a line employing an epistrophe: "Now I want you to remember that no bastard ever won a war by dying for his country. He won it by making the other poor dumb bastard die for his country."
- **Assonance**—Assonance is a certain form of repetitive expression where the speaker successively uses different words with similar vowel sounds. Johnny Cochran, speaking in the closing arguments of the O.J. Simpson trial, famously used assonance in his unforgettable line, "The gloves didn't fit. If it doesn't fit, you must acquit."
- **Anadiplosis**—Anadiplosis is repeating the last word or phrase at or near the beginning of the next sentence, phrase, or clause. "They call for you. The general who became a slave; the slave who became a gladiator; the gladiator who defied an Emperor. Striking story." (Joaquin Phoenix in *Gladiator.*)
- **Scesis onomaton**—Scesis onomaton is actually another of my favorites. It's the use of different words that say the same thing, successively. When you use this technique, you can try a "ladder" approach. Speak each word/phrase successively louder with a crescendo on the last one. Two great examples are:
  - "For whatever reasons, Ray, call it fate; call it luck; call it karma. I believe that everything happens for a reason." (Bill Murray in *Ghost Busters.*)
  - "Four years ago, Jimmy Swaggart said this about us: He said 'This here song by the Police, Murder by Numbers, was written by Satan. Performed by the Sons of Satan . . . Beelzebub! . . .

Lucifer! . . . The Horned One!!'" (Sting, from the band The Police, at a concert. He was introducing the song "Murder by Numbers" that they were about to sing. Now this one is really worth listening to, to hear the ladder delivery he uses. But it's also fun because they employ a drum roll after each key word. Of course, we don't normally get to use drums in our speeches, but the effect is pretty great.)

There are other types of repetition that you can use as well (see AmericanRhetoric.com as I mentioned above for a full list with definitions and audio samples). The point is, repetition can be a very useful tool, especially when wielded skillfully and with purpose.

So use it and use it well (except at oral argument, where you'll drive your judge or justices nuts).

Antithesis

Antithesis is a wonderful and very common rhetorical tool that can be employed effectively to contrast two opposing ideas, outcomes, or situations. You probably use antithetical phrases on a daily basis. Here are a few memorable uses of this tool:

- "In criminal law you see bad people on their best day. In family law you see good people on their worst day." (Anonymous).
- "People don't care how much you know until they know how much you care." (John C. Maxwell)
- "Communication is speaking so people listen and listening so people speak." (John Davies, Davies! Public Affairs)
- "The weaker the argument, the stronger the words." (Anonymous)
- "Don't let what you can't do stop you from doing what you can do." (John Wooden)
- "If we try, we might succeed; if we do not try, we cannot succeed." (Anonymous).

And of course this topic cannot go without listing one of the most famous uses of antithesis in the latter half of the twentieth century, "Ask not what your country can do for you, but what you can do for your country." (John F. Kennedy, Inauguration speech, 1961).

IMAGE/DELIVERY

CHAPTER SIX

Your Image Does Matter

I will never forget the day I went to a continuing legal education presentation and a respected, experienced female attorney took off her sandals, sat barefoot in a seat right in front of the first audience member, and gave her presentation. Oh, and she wasn't wearing a suit either—just a camisole tank top and slacks. Seriously? *Seriously?*

Do I even need to analyze what is wrong with this picture? What do you think her audience was thinking when it was actually happening?

First impressions are made faster than ever before.

Many years ago, when I began asking audience members how long they thought it took to make a first impression, they would usually shout out some length of time between one and five minutes. In the mid-2000s the answer shortened to between one and two minutes. In the late-2000s the audience usually shouted out variants of *seconds*—"five seconds," "ten seconds," "thirty seconds." And since about 2010 or so, we're down to one to five seconds. Sometimes I hear "instantaneously" and a few times I even heard "a nanosecond." Star Trek, here I come.

This trend in my audience's response is telling—they now feel the amount of time it takes to make a first impression is startlingly short.

And they're not wrong. In 2003, a release from PR Web said that "[p]sychologists, writers and seminar leaders caution that you only have seven to 17 seconds of interacting with strangers before they form an opinion of you." More recently, Malcolm Gladwell, author of *Blink: The Power of Thinking Without Thinking,* reported that the decisions may occur much faster—**think instantaneously or in a couple of seconds.**

In the last few decades, people have become more judgmental, more critical, and much quicker to make assumptions about a person. The communications and PR professionals I speak with attribute this to not just information overload but also, more likely, our instant gratification and media-saturated society. We are used to life in thirty-second sound bytes and 140-character tweets—our subconscious adjusts to information input accordingly.

And the younger the audience—the audience that has been brought up on YouTube, Vimeo, Twitter, and the latest app—the more critically they will view the visual input they receive.

What does this mean to the speaker? It means you don't get a grace period. You don't get to stroll into a room or a courtroom, ignore your audience, sit on a dais, shuffle your papers, clear your throat, play with your microphone, or chat with your co-presenters/co-counsel without ever looking at your audience, judge, or jury—not without them judging you the entire time.

Yikes!:

An appellate justice who heard about my book told me a funny story recently about something that had just happened in his courtroom. There was an attorney arguing in front of the justice and the attorney started off with "Judge Segal," pronouncing the name "Se Gall" (like the actor Steven Segal). What's wrong with this picture? First, the attorney was in front of a Justice, not a Judge. And second, Justice Segal's last name is pronounced "See Gul" not "Se Gall." So not only did the attorney call Justice Segal "Judge," he also mispronounced the name. Yikes! Not a great way to make a first impression.

Because you want to be building your credibility and your likeability from the moment your audience sees you, you have to pay attention to everything the moment you walk into the room, not the moment you start speaking. You have to pay attention to your image before you leave your home or office. This means you have to think about what you're going to wear—preferably before you are standing naked in front of your closet so you still have time to go get a suit that fits or a new top, tie, or shoes (or run out and pick up your suit at the dry cleaners because you forgot to do it earlier).

This also means you have to have your papers organized and ready to use (not in a folder) before you walk into the room or up to the dais. It means you have to ensure you are using good posture—no slumping—and it means you want to immediately start greeting and nodding and smiling at/with your audience the moment you walk into the room—in any setting, courtroom or not.

Your Presence Is Doing the Talking

As a speaker, you want to cultivate a likeable, confident presence. Good old Merriam-Webster defines "presence" as the "bearing, carriage, or air of a person; *especially* stately or distinguished bearing." It is "a noteworthy quality of poise and effectiveness."

In other words, your presence is your persona—the impression you give off. Your presence affects your audience's ability to like you, respect you, and believe in what you have to say. If you are off-putting, arrogant, sloppy, overly nervous, unsure of yourself, or merely a bit scattered, your audience will notice long before you actually start speaking.

One way to cultivate a likeable, confident presence is to practice public speaking as much as possible in nonthreatening settings. I highly recommend spending six to twelve months as part of a local Toastmasters group that meets at least once a month (Toastmasters.com). Started in 1905, Toastmasters is an international organization with multiple chapters virtually everywhere. For example, within twenty-five miles of Pasadena, California, there are almost 400 chapters. When you belong to a chapter, you deliver presentations regularly to a supportive audience. Over time, the feedback and practice pay off. It is a fantastic way to gain public speaking experience, especially if you don't have a lot of opportunities via work or home and are terrified of the few times you do have to speak.

Toastmasters gives you the ability to make mistakes in a nonthreatening environment, and it gives you a chance to work on developing a likeable, confident presence when speaking, through practice, practice, practice. I highly recommend it for anyone who wants to get better at speaking and especially for anyone who has any fear of public speaking.

The following are some other areas you can control right now, to help develop a likeable, confident presence.

Your Attire

Every now and then someone rolls his or her eyes when I discuss how a person should dress when speaking in public, especially in a courtroom, as if this topic was so elementary that it was insulting. Now, normally I'd agree. But in reality, I can't. In some instances, dress issues when speaking in public can be attributed to the lack of training in younger generations, but it is not simply an age-related problem. I see people of all ages dressing inappropriately when presenting . . . *all* the time.

So, if you're a skeptic (and even if you are not), you'll want to take note. A while back there was an article in a popular legal blog that discussed a recent bench-bar meeting in the Seventh Circuit that eventually devolved into a good-natured complain-fest about the way attorneys dress in the courtroom.

Here are a few of the choice comments:

> One U.S. District Court Judge had an issue with a woman who had shown up for a court hearing in attire that looked as though she had stopped in "on her way home from the gym."
>
> A Bankruptcy Judge who presides in the Northern District of Illinois said that male attorneys who come before him with wacky ties, like those with lots of smiley faces, also cross the line of appropriateness.
>
> "You don't dress in court as if it's Saturday night and you're going out to a party," said another judge from the audience. "Dress as a serious person who takes the court seriously."
>
> A partner from a law firm recalled how jurors in one of his cases were fixated on a trial lawyer's "argyle socks."

(Lynne Marek, Federal Judges Grouse About Lawyers' Courtroom Attire, May 21, 2009, National Law Journal)

The rule of thumb is that you should always dress a notch better than you think your audience will be dressed. You can always dress it down once you get there if you feel uncomfortable. For example, you can always take off your suit jacket or tie, and you can always roll up your sleeves.

You want to pay attention to the speaking setting and who your audience is. That means you will always wear a business suit in the courtroom—any courtroom setting. Not business casual, not a sports jacket, not a dress that could be worn out to a club, not summer sandals—a business suit, with the appropriate shoes and accouterments. If it is a long trial, you have to decide your strategy regarding how you will dress—based on the makeup of the jury—and the impression you want to make day after day.

Trial Tip:

Many trial attorneys and jury consultants recommend wearing the same suit each day and only changing your shirt (and for men, your tie). Again, this depends on the setting, the trial, and the jury.

Outside of the courtroom, your dress depends on your audience, as mentioned. If it is a business presentation, a business suit is appropriate. If you are at a casual church or temple function, you may wear khakis and a nice shirt or blouse. If you are speaking to a group of high school or college kids, you'll want to dress it down, so you are not intimidating or worse. If you're in Hawaii, your attire will likely be more casual, even at a business event, than in New York, or even Los Angeles. But even in Hawaii, I wouldn't recommend a sundress or shorts.

If you are tempted to dress casually because you are super successful and you don't care, or you don't think your audience cares, think again. They do care, and they will judge you—even if you're Barbara Walters or David Boies. There is only one Steve Jobs. Except, perhaps, Tim Cook (Apple's CEO post Steve Jobs).

A friend of mind once told me about a colleague of his who is very well known in the legal community, well respected, and seen as the "go-to guy" regarding his field of expertise that provides services to lawyers and law firms. Let's call "the guy" John. John gives a ton of talks all over the country at legal events. He is undoubtedly one of the top experts in his area. But John never bothers to put on a suit. Sometimes he even wears flip-flops, and he always wears jeans.

One day my friend was sitting in the audience—a very large audience—at a national legal event, and his colleague John was speaking. My friend noticed that the female attorney sitting next to him wasn't paying any attention to the speaker, so he asked her what she thought of John. "This guy? He's a joke. I've seen him speak before. Look at how he's dressed! He always looks that way . . . . "

It always matters what you are wearing, how you look, and how you hold yourself.

First and foremost—in *any* speaking situation—here's your mantra:

You want people paying attention to what you are saying, not what you are wearing (unless you're in the fashion industry perhaps).

Here are some basic guidelines:

Tips for Everyone:

- Wear dark or dark-toned suits, such as charcoal, brown, olive, dark blue, black, or gray. If you want to go the extra mile, find out what colors work best with your skin tones and hair.

Example:

I use professional costumers from the entertainment industry to periodically choose my suits and keep me on track with complementary colors. When I was younger I wore a lot of black suits and white tops. Now I wear brown suits, dark gray suits with blue pinstripes, dark blue suits, all of various textures and tones. The shirts/blouses that I wear with my suits are always blue, violet, coral, or pink. And when I look at video from various speeches, it's pretty clear the brown suits with coral tops work *a lot* better than the previously used black suits with white tops.

Obviously, you don't need to go to this length if you only speak every now and then, but if you are in court all the time, or speak frequently for marketing and business development, or because it's your job, you might want to consider hiring a professional (who knows professional attire) to help you.

- White and pastel suits convey a certain image—spring, soft, etc. They may sometimes be appropriate—say for a mother-daughter spring function at which you are speaking. But they are never appropriate in a business speaking situation.
- Soft-colored suits or slacks and sport coat combinations—tans, for example—may work at a church function, a high school reunion, or some other speaking setting. But again, in a business setting, and in court, they do not convey enough professionalism. It's a social perception issue, at least in the United States.
- Generally speaking, everyone looks better with a colored shirt under their suit rather than stark white. You want the color on the inside (the shirt), not the outside (the suit), as the color draws people's eyes toward your face—which is where your message is coming from. This doesn't mean you can't wear a white shirt in the courtroom. It just means colored shirts don't wash out skin tones the way white shirts do.
- Nothing you'd wear out for a night on the town is appropriate (yes, this needs to be said and applies to men and women both).
- Manicured nails (if nails are messy).
- Hair should be neat, unobtrusive, out of your face and eyes.
- No flashy jewelry of any kind should be worn.

Tips for Women:

- **Makeup**—Not over the top. Think: "What would I wear makeup-
  and attire-wise if I was a reporter interviewing the President of
  the United States?"
- **Skirts**—Not too short. This is important enough to repeat—**no
  short skirts**. Yes, it's a problem.
- **Shirts/blouses**—No shirts or blouses that show too much skin
  (low v-neck, tummy, or top, or see-through).
- **Nails**—No outrageous nail polish colors or nails so long they
  scare people.
- **Jewelry**—Worth mentioning again, no flashy jewelry of any kind
  (it's distracting).
- **Shoes**—Avoid spiked heels and the latest platform shoes. Avoid
  open-toed or "peep-toed" shoes, sandals, or shoes that look like you're
  headed for a night on the town or a day at the beach. Think "classy
  pump" and you're safe. It doesn't have to be boring, just professional.

What's your mantra again?

*You want people paying attention to what you are saying, not what you
are wearing.* Is this seriously worth arguing about?

The big debate: Skirt suits vs. pantsuits. When it comes to attire, I
always get one question from a woman at my presentation skills programs:
"When in court, should I wear a skirt, or can I wear pants?" It's a sad commentary on society, but it is a somewhat important question, and it isn't
something that is taught in law school or at law firms.

So, in answer to the universal question (skirt suit or pantsuit in court),
it boils down to this: "Who is in your audience?" Are you appearing before
an older judge? Do you have a jury that is composed mainly of older, retired
people? If the answer to either question is yes, go with the conservative,
professional skirt suit to be safe.

The older generation still expects women to be dressed in skirt suits;
they grew up in an era in which pantsuits were inappropriate. Because
you can't change inherent feelings and biases such as these, and frankly
that's not your job when you are in court, the smarter course is to choose
the professional skirt suit, at an appropriate length, with appropriate high
heels. Eventually this will no longer be something that matters as this older
generation becomes too old to be seated in a jury box or on a bench.

Oh, and forget what you see on television.

I will say it again: *you want your audience paying attention to what you are saying, not what you are wearing.*

Tips for Men:

- **Ties**—Wear a nice flattering color that works with your suit and shirt. If you don't know what that means, watch a few political speeches by any modern president. Your ties don't have to be ugly and they don't have to be red or blue, but you need to avoid wearing a distracting tie.

  Ditch the sports ties, ties with political message, holiday ties, ties made by your kids for Father's Day. You want to wear something nice, but not something so flashy or distracting that people are paying attention to your tie instead of your words. Judges really do complain about this.
- **Shoes**—Make sure they are polished and have no holes in the bottoms. Yep.
- **Jewelry**—Avoid large flashy watches and rings.

The bottom line is, you guessed it: *you want your audience paying attention to what you are saying, not what you are wearing.*

CHAPTER SEVEN

Pitch-Perfect Delivery

Everyone has their own style of speaking in public. And while different settings might call for different approaches (changes in tone or in seriousness), the same "persona" is usually present with each speaker. Think of the great public speakers of the past fifty years (a number of presidents and candidates might spring to mind). When you think of their speeches and how effective they were, you can see that they all managed to project a positive image of themselves and their own charismatic persona.

There are several tried-and-true delivery techniques that are guaranteed to improve your delivery style and the impact you have on an audience—any audience.

Let's get started.

Eye Contact Means Everything

Making eye contact with your audience throughout your entire presentation is **the number one way** you can improve your delivery style.

Eye contact is the primary way to connect with your audience. It enhances your presence. It makes you appear confident, credible, and in control. A speaker who studiously reads from prepared remarks and rarely looks up to the audience can be seen as either shifty, boring, or both. The simple rule is: *talk directly to people and they will listen to you.*

So how do you do it? To begin with, let's start with the size of your audience. If it is small (fewer than fifty people or so), you will find many opportunities to make eye contact with virtually every member of your audience. As you speak, vary your eye contact with different parts of the room. In other words, make sure you **don't focus on one side only,** which I've seen speakers do time and again.

Additionally, try to avoid focusing on that one person in the audience to whom you will naturally gravitate. That's usually the one person who gives you positive nonverbal feedback. I call them "friendly faces."

While you do want to make eye contact with friendly faces throughout your presentation (better than looking at the guy reading the paper), you don't want to focus on just one person. Why? Because over time, you will begin to make that person feel really uncomfortable. Nobody likes being the center of attention for too long if they're not asking for it. What's more, the rest of the audience will be saying, "What about us? We have needs too." The remainder of the audience will eventually tune you out as you will appear to be having your own private conversation with that one person.

If you have a larger audience, it will be impossible for you to make eye contact with everyone, but that's not a problem. The solution is to divide the audience into sections. Mentally split the group into four or six or whatever number of different sections. Within each section, seek out the one or two people who have "friendly faces." Once you do, everyone else near that person will think that you're looking at them. It has to do with depth perception.

The best way to explain it is via analogy: Have you ever been walking down the street and somebody waves to you or starts speaking and you don't know who they are? Then right when you're going to respond (or sometimes after), you discover they're actually targeting the person behind you? That's what I'm talking about here. If you look at those one or two people within that section, everyone else in their vicinity will think you're making eye contact with them.

Once you've established your mental sections and found the friendly faces to address, you'll want to vary it throughout the room. This should be done randomly, not systematically. (You don't want to look like a robot: "Now I look left. Now I look right. Now I look left again.") Make a personal connection with your audience. Use eye contact to engage in a dialogue or a conversation with as many of them as you can.

As you proceed, you should attempt to adjust your presentation depending on the feedback that you're getting. If you're getting the "I am lost" look, go back and re-explain. If you're getting the "I'm so bored I've gone off to la-la land" look from your audience, you need to take the time to re-engage your listeners. Some of the ways you can do this are by varying your vocals, moving around the room, asking questions of your audience, or inviting them to ask questions of you. You can also make a self-deprecating joke. For example, once recently when I spoke at a law firm "lunch and learn," I couldn't get the attorneys to answer my questions. So at some point I said, "Okay, that's it, I'm going home." It got a lot of laughs and they started answering my questions.

If you're asking them questions to get them engaged again, offering a reward of chocolate or Starbucks cards when they ask or answer a question doesn't hurt either (obviously in an out-of-court setting). Yes, this really works. Especially after lunch.

A final word about eye contact: It can sometimes be distracting to the speaker. You look up, you find a friendly face and . . . the person you see suddenly reminds you of your first-grade teacher. Or an in-law. Or your mailman. And in that moment, that brief second of distraction, your brain can be jolted and your train of thought can derail. Prepare for this. Know that even if you were to look up and see Santa Claus staring back at you, you could keep going without batting an eye.

I repeat it here because it cannot be overstated: **Eye contact is, and will remain, the single best way to engage an audience.**

Energy Is Good. Energy Is *Great!*

It is amazing how many speakers appear bored when making a presentation. There they are, up in front of a crowd or jury, with the golden opportunity to impart knowledge, create excitement, persuade in favor of their client, or convince the group to embrace a new idea, and yet . . . they look as if they'd rather be almost anywhere else. Bored. Listless. Resentful.

You don't have to be a motivational speaker to have permission to be passionate and enthusiastic about your topic. If you're excited about what you have to say, *show it*. If, on the other hand, you do *not* have the requisite passion or enthusiasm for your particular topic (but you have to deliver the speech anyway), there's only one thing to do: *fake it.*

Yes, I really mean that. *Fake it till you make it.*

Of course, if you're not engaged and interested in your topic, you probably shouldn't be making the presentation in the first place, but there are many times when speakers, lawyers, and supervisors are forced to make speeches against their will or in front of a jury with bad facts or an unlikeable client. In those instances, if the choice is between showing your lack of enthusiasm or displaying an enthusiasm that you don't really feel: *Fake. It.*

Energy is contagious, yes. But the reverse is also true. If you can't muster any energy or enthusiasm for your presentation, how do you expect anyone else to?

Let me use my own experience as an example. I teach my three-hour in-depth seminar on public speaking to law firms, corporate executive groups, businesses, bar groups, associations, public agencies, and the like. I fly all over the country to do this. And when I do it, no matter where I am, I am "on" for all three hours.

Lack of sleep? Jet lag? Small or unappreciative crowd? It doesn't matter. I smile, jump up in front of the group, and let 'em have it with both barrels. Even the most listless crowd will perk up if you attack your subject with gusto, and there is no better way to win them over than to get them to enjoy something they start off thinking they're going to hate.

So, what happens after the program is over? As you'd expect, I crash like a diabetic going into sugar shock. I'm so exhausted after these sessions I no longer schedule anything afterwards because I know I won't have the energy to participate. I always find that I have used it up in the program. Why go to such lengths and put myself in such a state? Because it works. I *repeatedly* get comments about how exciting these programs are and how enthusiastic I appear to be.

And you know what? Even though I love teaching this seminar and I love the topic itself, there are times when I wake up at 6:00 A.M. (an ungodly hour on any day) and think to myself, "Why am I doing this? I'm tired. I don't want to do this." It doesn't happen often, but with my travel schedule and running a business, it happens.

Yet when the time comes, I still turn it on for the presentation. And on the rare occasion when I have run out of steam in the last twenty minutes or so, it inevitably comes up in the evaluations. Audiences notice.

So, if you want your audience to believe that you're a good speaker and to hear what you have to say, you *must* be energetic. Give yourself the permission to show enthusiasm and get excited about your topic. Trust me—it's contagious.

A word about the courtroom. Judges get bored. Juries get bored. Being enthusiastic and committed to your client in this setting is just as important as any other setting. You aren't going to go over the top and present like a motivational speaker, but you still need to present with energy.

The Problem with Podiums

When you arrive at virtually any speaking venue—from a meeting room to a convention hall—the organizers will more likely than not have provided you with a podium. They believe that, by doing so, they are doing you a favor. And while a podium can be a useful item at times (for setting your notes or drink upon), they can also be terribly misused. And if you believe that delivering your speech from behind that podium is going to get your audience to react to you in a positive way, please read this next sentence very carefully: *When it comes to podiums, think **anchor** and **barrier**.* A podium can be either one. As an *anchor*, it is helpful to be able to return to it, lean on it, or refer to your notes if you're moving on to a new topic and need to have your next point brought to mind. But whatever you do, do *not* think of your podium as being the place from which to deliver your speech. Because it can also be a *barrier*.

Placing a large block of wood between you and your audience is the surest way to distance yourself from them and from you. Yes, it is comforting to have that buffer between the two of you, but you shouldn't be in search of comfort. You should be searching for a *connection,* and you're not going to connect with anyone from behind a shield like that. Remember that what shields you from the audience also shields *them* from *you.*

What I always advise speakers to do when they arrive at a space and find themselves with a podium is to try to make sure it is pushed just a little bit to the side. Not completely off the stage, of course—you'll still want to use it for your notes and a drink of water—but just far enough away so that it does not otherwise impede your movement. Because movement is one of the key elements in how to bring your audience closer to you.

In the last section, we talked about energy. If you want to display energy and enthusiasm to your audience, however, how do you do such a thing standing behind a podium? You don't. You have to *step out,* move around, and put your entire persona on display.

Presuming you know your topic well enough to only refer to your notes occasionally, you'll find that walking away from the podium is a freeing experience. It allows you to use both hands to gesture, to keep your feet moving and your blood pumping. It gives the audience something to watch besides a head suspended above a lectern.

So, when it's the right setting, request a lavalier microphone (lapel microphone) so that you *can* walk around—if the only mike is the one on the podium, it is pretty hard to do that.

Your movements and gestures once you have walked away from the podium do not need to be rehearsed in advance, but you should try moving around and delivering your speech beforehand anyway just to get used to the idea of being untethered. You don't have to think "I'm going to walk to my left during this section and walk toward them during this part," though.

Try to let your movements be more organic and natural and the audience will sense that you are relaxed and delivering your speech with confidence.

You also want to guard against getting *too* enthusiastic and moving around too much. You can only watch a butterfly for so long before you get dizzy. Keep your movements and your gestures economical but not stiff. It may take you a while to be totally comfortable talking without the podium as a crutch, but the benefits are undeniable.

Suddenly, you appear more credible. Your confidence level appears to soar. You immediately gain the trust of your audience because you're really talking to them, not lecturing them. Freely moving around the space and delivering your speech in a more natural fashion is much, *much* better than a monotone recitation. Try it and see.

During those times when you are *forced* to use a podium, do what you can to engage your audience vocally or physically anyway (even standing to the side of the podium is better than behind it). No matter what the situation, do what you can to minimize the sense that there is something between you and your audience. They will thank you for it with their undivided attention.

If, however, you're in a courtroom, you almost always have to be behind a podium. At these times, try to stand a little to either side so you aren't completely blocked.

If you're in the rare courtroom where your judge lets you walk around in trial, do it. But do it slowly and purposefully. And, of course, don't stand too close to the jury box.

Gesture Like You Mean It

Among the many difficulties faced by powerful public speakers, none is more confounding than the age-old question—"What do I do with my hands?"

It would be easy to say, "Let your hands do whatever they want." But in truth, there are some simple guidelines that can help you develop natural and expressive gestures while you speak.

And let's be clear: Gesturing while you speak is a very good thing. It is one of the most helpful ways of expressing to your audience that you have energy and enthusiasm for the subject at hand. A speaker who stands stock-still at the podium or on the stage is signaling to their audience that they would rather be anywhere else but where they are. It's also boring.

That said, there are also some pitfalls to gesturing while you speak. For one thing, you don't want to be overly repetitive in your gestures. Speakers can sometimes make the mistake of punching the air every few seconds or pointing over and over again; these are gestures that can mesmerize audience members (and put them to sleep).

Another gesture that has become endemic among public speakers is a thing I call "The Clinton." President Bill Clinton—who is easily one of the greatest public speakers of the past century—developed a closed-fist hand gesture that has become uniquely associated with him. If you've seen him speak, you've seen this gesture. Unfortunately, perhaps because of his great success on the public stage, this gesture has been adopted by speakers all across the world in an attempt to emulate him. Take it from me—leave this one alone. It just looks silly.

Just because you've been advised to move, don't let attempting to do so cause your body to tense up and your gestures to become tight and stiff. In other words, don't be mechanical. Nobody listens to a robot.

One common bit of advice you'll sometimes hear, and I'd like to dispel, is the old story that attorneys should not gesture in court, at oral argument or in front of a jury. I can't tell you the number of times I've heard from young associates that a wise old mentor told them that they should minimize or completely eliminate their gesturing in a courtroom setting. This is wrong, wrong, *wrong*.

I'm not saying you need to do jumping jacks, but you cannot abandon your natural movement just because you happen to be standing in front of a judge or jury. If you feel the urge to gesture while making your argument, do it.

The rule of thumb—and it's a simple one—is this: Natural is best. Use whatever movements work for your body. Truth is, the less you think about it, the more natural it will look. If you find yourself suddenly hyper-aware of your gesturing, try to concentrate on something else (the subject of your presentation would be a good idea). If you're not thinking about your hands, they'll generally take care of themselves.

However, if you find yourself not gesturing at all and this is impeding your delivery, you can put one hand in your pocket and it will redirect some energy to the one free hand, which will—all on its own—begin to gesture more. Generally speaking, though, keep your hands out of your pockets.

Vocal Dynamics

Knowing what to do with your voice is key to communicating your message. If you have read this far, you have picked up valuable tips on your image and audience connection. But if you can't be clearly understood, or if you deliver your entire presentation in an unvarying monotone, you'll be wasting a lot of effort and wondering why your presentations don't have enough impact. Make your voice and your inflection work for you! Here are a few aspects of your vocal performance you won't want to miss:

Vary Your Vocals

Ask your average person on the street what they find to be the most annoying vocal habit public speakers fall into and they'll say the same thing: a *monotone*. Droning on and on, without any inflection or change in tone, is indeed the surest way to get an audience to tune you out.

This would be a very short section if speaking in a monotone were the *only* vocal sin that a public speaker can commit, but unfortunately there are many others. Each of these mistakes stems from the same root cause: lack of variety. But an unvaried monotone is the first one people name.

Tune Your Tone

This follows on the heels of the monotone issue. Everyone has a natural tone range that they call upon when speaking. When you get excited, your tone may rise; when calm, it may slip half an octave or so. But generally, as you pass through your day, you rely on the same few notes in your vocal range to express yourself.

When speaking before a group, however, you should take care to modulate and change your vocal range whenever possible. This may happen naturally due to the fact that you are likely trying to project your voice further than you normally do, but if you're using a microphone, it is very easy to slip into a safe, narrow, and ultimately very *boring* tonality.

To combat this, and to even know it is an issue, when you practice your speech take the time to audio record yourself on your smartphone or other device and play portions of your speech back for yourself. Most people don't like the sound of their own voice anyway, but listen for as long as you can, paying particular attention to your range. Is it flat? Do you have natural highs and lows? Do you need to warm up before you begin speaking to open up your lungs and your nasal passages, to get your lips and tongue moving?

Don't be afraid to be critical of your voice, but not to the point where it causes you to doubt your abilities. Anyone can expand his or her vocal range with practice, and if you already enjoy a wide range of tones, you've got a head start.

Moving around and having enthusiasm for your topic and presentation are two of the most natural ways to enhance your vocal variety and avoid a monotone. It's hard to be monotone if you are excited about your presentation.

Adjust the Volume

As with tone, your volume can get stuck at a certain level (like a car stuck in first gear) and you might find it difficult to alter your level so that it rises and falls naturally. When you keep your volume at the same level, you are in just as much danger of lulling your audience to sleep as you are with a monotone.

Luckily, the two tend to go hand-in-hand. If you are varying your vocal tone, your volume should also decrease and increase at the same time. But if you find this is not the case when you review the tapes of your speech, an important tip is to remember that the microphone is there not simply to project your voice but also to *support* your voice. You still have to get the words out and into your audience's ears, and your volume should not be determined by the A/V person twisting a knob on the amplifier.

Stay well back from the microphone when you're speaking and try to *project*. Don't yell, mind you. Sending your voice out loud and clear doesn't mean yelling. It means sending your voice out at a *slightly* louder level than your normal speaking voice. If you can do that and still vary it up and down depending on where you are in the speech, your audience will tend to stay engaged.

Adjusting your vocal volume also helps you deliver your presentation with impact. And it helps you get back those folks who might be wandering off. When your vocals go softer, it signals to your audience to pay attention, something important is being said. We all want to hear whatever is being whispered nearby. When you go louder, you are also signaling to your audience to pay attention! Just in a different manner.

You don't want to deliver your entire speech softly, nor do you want to do the whole thing with a loud voice. Either will be difficult for your audience to pay attention to for very long. So vary your vocals, the key word being "vary."

How Many Words per Minute?

When human beings get excited, they tend to speak at a much faster rate than usual. Conversely, when bored or laconic (or when they really want to emphasize a point), people will reduce their rate of speech considerably. Changing the speed at which you deliver your presentation is yet another way to keep things lively and interesting.

Of course, that also means policing yourself carefully. Are you speaking so quickly that people cannot take in what you're saying? Are you delivering too much of your speech in One. Word. Sentences. Pausing. Between. Each. One? It is entirely possible to overemphasize just as it is easy to over-enunciate (see below).

One of the ways you'll know you are speaking too fast is if you start tripping over your words or mispronouncing them. It's a problem I have, and when I start tripping over my words I know I am going too fast. If this happens to you a lot, write "Slow down" on your notes on every page in a visible manner. The reminder every time you look at your notes will help you get it under control.

You will, under most circumstances, speak at your natural speed of delivery, but throwing your audience a curveball once in a while by varying the rate of your presentation will help immeasurably in keeping the audience on their toes.

And, like varying the volume, it is an effective way to get your audience's attention and signal to them that something is important—if you do it intentionally, for effect, and briefly. For example, rattling off statistics somewhat quickly, and then repeating the last, most important one slowly, will grab their attention and make them listen, as I mentioned previously.

Enunciate! Articulate!

So you're speaking before a group and you're using a varied tone, altering your volume for emphasis, and changing the pace occasionally to add pleasant elements of drama. Everything seems to be going fine. Except one small thing: You're mumbling, and no one can make out quite what you're saying.

Enunciation (properly and clearly pronouncing your words) and articulation (expressing entire thoughts clearly) are two peas in the same pod. Be *very* sure that you are properly pronouncing every word in your speech, paying careful attention to proper names, medical and technical terminology, and words from another language. You don't want to sound like a rube in the big city trying out a fancy new word and mispronouncing it.

And be sure you are doing so clearly. And for those of you who speak quickly, pay close attention to this one—it is easy to stumble over your words.

But assuming you know how to properly pronounce every word you plan to deliver, you must also be able to articulate the thoughts that are connected to the words. Some speakers can begin a point and then meander off, getting lost even before they reach the end of a sentence. Know where you are going and how you are planning to get there and try to stay the course as much as possible.

Pausing Without . . . Um . . . Blowing It

We all know that "ums" are bad and that the best way to get rid of them is just to do it. Pausing silently for effect, however, is extremely effective. Finding the right moment to pause has a way of drawing an audience into a speech like no other tool.

Inserting a short pause after an important sentence is an effective and subtle way to tell your audience that what you just said is of the utmost importance and they should take a moment and think about it.

When you rush past all your points (like John Kerry did in his DNC nomination speech in 2004), nothing resonates. The point you were trying to make cannot be absorbed. Just as important, when you pause intentionally, it sends a signal to your audience on a subconscious level. They will pay more attention to you without even knowing they're doing it.

You can also use pauses to signal that what you are *about* to say is important as well. Pausing at the right moment (at the climax of a story or when you're ready to make an important point) can create suspense that draws your audience to you. They will know that something worthwhile is about to be said and they will imperceptibly lean forward to hear you make it.

In other words, you can pause after a point or before a point for the same effect.

As with every tool, pausing can be both misused and overused. Some speakers make the mistake of being too reliant on notes and inserting pauses where they make no sense. Looking down, losing your place, or trying to recall a specific point will chop up a speech into pieces that do not resonate at all. When you pause, your audience wants to know why. If you don't have a reason, you're just confusing them. Pausing like this lacks pace, flow, and purpose and it sucks the life out of a speech.

Purposeful, powerful pauses (if you'll forgive the alliteration) can make or break your speech. Hitting a pause at just the right moment with just the right amount of emphasis can leave your audience literally breathless. They will gasp, their eyes will widen, and you will see your point land (okay, they might not actually gasp and maybe their eyes won't widen, but you will definitely see your point land).

When you get it right, you'll know that your words are going to stay with them long after you're finished speaking.

So when it comes to pauses, use them and use them well.

Oops, sorry. I was supposed to actually pause for effect, not read the words "pause for effect" out loud. Okay, where were we?

Practice Makes . . . Well, You Know

There is no "easy" button when it comes to public speaking. Time and again speakers ask me how they can improve and then look at me funny when my answer is "Practice." It is clear that their look says "as if I have time."

The *only* way to become a better public speaker is to prepare in advance and practice. Eventually, you might be able to give a presentation without practicing first, but it is the rare speaker who has this gift. If they have it, it is usually because they are already well-practiced public speakers.

All too often, people wait until the last minute to create their presentation, leaving no time at all to practice and only enough time to worry. That is not a recipe for success, only disaster.

There are also those who believe that practice is beneath them and that they will do better if they just get up there and wing it. If this is you, you might want to rethink that strategy.

An important thing to note: Preparation is not a substitute for practice (and the reverse is not true either). You need to both prepare *and* practice.

As often as possible before delivering your presentation, find a place you can be alone (a closed office or your bedroom at home), place your notes in front of you, and deliver the speech exactly as you plan to do it. At full volume, if you can. Every time you run through the speech, it will improve. Guaranteed. And if you want to go the extra mile, video or audio record yourself while you practice. It might be a little hard to watch yourself afterwards, but it's how you'll learn if you have bad habits like saying "um," pacing, pausing too much, having a choppy delivery, playing with your jewelry, or any other distracting behavior.

It is time to dispel an old wives' tale. For decades people have been told to practice in front of a mirror. No! Don't do it! It will just distract you, and it's impossible to pay attention to what you are doing and saying while doing and saying it in front of a mirror.

Additional Tools

There are many other ways to keep your speech as varied and interesting as possible. Here are a couple:

- **Showing emotion**—This is a slippery slope, so be careful. But letting your audience get a sense that you feel strongly about something is sometimes a very good thing. You don't want to cry or get overemotional with your audience, but giving something extra emphasis to let your audience know how important a particular topic or thought is to you can be a very effective, powerful tool. Use this technique wisely and *rarely*.
- **Voices other than your own**—I have a method I use in my public speaking course where I play aloud examples of certain techniques I am attempting to impart to my audience. These can include clips from movies, parts of famous or iconic speeches, or simply classical references that serve my particular purpose. At these moments, the audiences visibly perk up and tune in to the new aural treat I am

providing while at the same time giving my point the extra attention it deserves. If you find that introducing other voices or quotes will assist you, don't be afraid to use them, whether audio or video.

Don't Leak Your Feelings

Your audience won't know you're nervous unless you tell them. Nervous speakers "leak" their nervousness through a variety of ways, including:

- Slapping a podium
- Pacing
- Rocking back and forth or side to side
- Tapping a pen
- Jingling change in their pocket
- Playing with a ring (men), earring, or hair (women)
- Saying "um" too often
- Blinking or smacking their lips
- Holding their notes where everyone can see their notes shaking
- And finally: *Telling the audience that they are nervous.* Yes, this actually happens. All the time.

So how do you plug up your leaky feelings? The first thing is to know you have one or more of these bad habits. You can find out by practicing in front of someone who will tell you, or video recording yourself (and actually watching the video when you're finished), as I just mentioned.

True story:

A retired judge recently told me about an experience he had when he was in the Office of Chief Counsel for the Department of the Treasury, many years before he became a judge. There was an oral argument training session for the attorneys in the office that was videotaped. The trainers replayed each video to the entire group of attorneys, who then were encouraged to point out the problems they saw.

The judge remembered that when the trainers played back the recording of the judge's argument, he saw that he was constantly playing with his mustache, rubbing his chin, crossing his fingers, and playing with his ring. This occurred many decades before he told me the story and he still remembered it—and noted that they were all annoying gestures of his that he would not have known about without the video recording and playback session.

Once you've identified these habits, write reminders on your notes to pay attention. Use the universal "no" sign as shorthand. The more you're conscious of what you're doing, the less you'll do it. But breaking bad habits takes time.

Leaking your feelings is symptomatic of someone who is unprepared and unpracticed. The more experience you have, the less your nervousness will be noticeable to your audience.

Of course, for people who are terrified of speaking, it is more than simply a lack of preparation or a bad habit. Fear affects even the most practiced speaker at times, and it can be a major stress-producer for less-experienced presenters. For that reason, it's worth dealing with in some depth. I've devoted the next chapter to fear and how to beat it. (See Chapter Eight.)

CHAPTER EIGHT

Overcoming Your Fear

We now arrive at the point in this book where we illustrate and address the greatest obstacle public speakers generally face: fear.

Fear comes in many shapes and sizes. It can come in the form of butterflies in the stomach, a quavering voice, a red face and chest, or a burst of flop-sweat across your brow. Fear can cause you to lose the power of speech, make you giggle inappropriately, or make your mind go blank. It can embarrass you, beat you down, and keep you awake at night. But anxiety about speaking doesn't need to conquer you or ruin your chances of delivering a great presentation. It's a very natural response shared by many people, including some of our greatest speakers and performers, who have learned how to lessen its effects, even if they can't banish it forever.

In other words, there are things that you can do to help yourself.

Own Your Fear

Half of the battle in overcoming fear is realizing that it may never entirely go away. This should, despite how it sounds, be a comforting thought. After all, if you actually believed that fear could be completely defeated and then, moments before you stepped in front of a judge or an audience, a shiver of fear ran up your spine, you might well panic. But knowing that your fear can be diminished, even if not driven away entirely, allows you to recognize, confront, and—eventually—minimize your fear.

That, after all, is the ultimate goal. Not to banish fear, but to make it so insignificant that it no longer impedes your ability to do your job. And the first step in minimizing your fear is to *own* it. Once you have dealt with that reality, you can begin the real work: getting to know where it comes from and what you can do to minimize it. Let's start with the first part . . .

Sources of Anxiety

It's helpful to do some self-assessment about where your jitters might be coming from. There can be many different points of origin: Which one of these sounds like your biggest problem?

- **Pessimistic attitude toward speaking**—Your negative perception and reaction to the situation you face is a source of anxiety (e.g., "I hate public speaking," "public speaking makes me so nervous," "I really don't want to do this," "I hate having to speak in front of people").
- **Inadequate preparation and practice**—While most attorneys would never dream of facing a jury without preparation and practice, many seem to think that appearing before a judge, public agency, commission, or in public, is different in this regard. They put off preparing and practicing until the last moment (and some may not even do that at all). Then they wonder why the act of speaking was so traumatic or unsuccessful.
- **Negative or insufficient experience**—Bad past experiences or lack of any experience can create stress. Believing you don't "have the gift" of public speaking is a misnomer. Most people don't. Speaking is an acquired skill like any other—cooking, golf, even training your dog. And remember, most people get at least a little nervous when they speak, even the professionals.
- **Too much attention**—Many people are comfortable in groups and do not like to stand out. Public speaking singles a person out for attention and the risk of embarrassment. No one likes to be judged and when you stand up to speak in public you feel like you are being judged—whether you are or not.
- **Unrealistic goals**—Research shows that people who set realistic goals for themselves are less anxious and more successful than their counterparts with unrealistic goals.
- **Inaccurate perception of the audience**—Many view speaking and the audience as a threat to their mental well-being. Many believe the audience is waiting for a blunder so they can make fun of the speaker, challenge him or her, try to grab attention, and so on. Yet, with rare exceptions, audiences want speakers to succeed and are silently rooting for them to do so. And many respect you for having the courage to speak in public.

18(!) Ways to Manage Your Fear

Once you've got a handle on where some of your problems are coming from, it's time to go to work on fixing things as best you can. Here are best practices that have come from prior professors, years of being a speaker and teaching others how to give the best presentations:

1. **Remember to think of your presentation as a conversation, not a performance**—If you reorient your perspective and stop thinking of your talks as performances that must be perfect, you can reduce your level of fear. The next time you have to speak, think about just talking with your audience about your topic in the way that you chat with friends or colleagues. Of course, you'll be a lot more organized than that, but in reality, good presentations are *modified conversations.*

2. **Develop an optimistic attitude toward speaking**—Again, view it as communication, rather than performance. Think about it being an opportunity to tell a story or to give your audience a worthwhile gift. Give them credit for their ability to appreciate what you have to say to them and the time you took to say it.

    The inverse of this is also true—don't catastrophize. Don't exaggerate the imagined impact if your presentation doesn't go well. There certainly may be something important depending on the success of your speech, but the more you dwell on a worst-case scenario, the more you risk it coming to pass, and the more you will dread speaking in the future.

3. **Don't put off your preparation**—Prepare well in advance of the actual speech (this includes finding your supporting material, writing your outline, and practicing). And remember—you're the expert!

    Inexperienced speakers usually need more time than they think they do. And people who fear public speaking are the most likely to put off preparing for it. We are all great at procrastinating when it comes to something we don't want to do.

    Yet this is a recipe for disaster. The longer you wait, the more your anxiety and fear will build and the less likely you will have enough time to prepare and practice. Then when you finally deliver your presentation, you don't do as well as you could have and you create a self-fulfilling prophesy: "See, I am a horrible public speaker. That's why I hate it so much."

    It is a form of self-sabotage that reinforces your fear. Next time, no matter how hard it is for you, prepare far enough in advance that you have time to tinker with your speech, maybe do more research to clear up a point, read your briefs, cases, facts, the record, and whatever else you need to do to prepare, and as I have mentioned throughout, practice.

This is one of the best ways to reduce your fear, if not eliminate it altogether.

4. **Practice, practice, practice**—You are less likely to make a mistake if you are prepared and have worked out the kinks. Having practiced a few times reduces anxiety. Practicing in front of someone a final time is also hard, but it is a terrific way to help reduce your anxiety. At least someone has seen it first.

5. **Look for opportunities to gain speaking experience**—Speak for social or community groups whenever possible. Check out the list of nonthreatening opportunities in the next subsection. Instead of avoiding speaking, seek it out for the practice and experience. Remember, in most instances audiences want you to succeed; they are not gunning for you.

6. **Set realistic goals**—No one is perfect. Aim for improvement on specific or general areas—not perfection. Take one or two things in this book and incorporate them into your preparation or delivery—rhetorical devices, more eye contact, consciously choosing your organizational pattern—whatever—and see how that goes. Then build upon your success by using new techniques each time. And setting realistic goals each time.

7. **Adopt constructive behaviors**—When it is possible, pick a topic you know about and like (be sure it will serve your audience). This reduces anxiety. The more you know your topic, the easier it is to speak about it and the less nervous you will be.

8. **Realize the audience wants you to succeed**—Your perception of the audience will affect the level of fear you feel. If you think of them as wanting to be there and being supportive of you, it will be much easier to deliver your speech than if you think of them as the enemy. In most instances, your audience will be empathetic. And most audiences hate to see speakers fail or be uncomfortable, because it makes audience members uncomfortable.

9. **Identify with your listeners**—Use "us" language, not "you" or "them." Think of yourself as a member of the audience, part of the group, with at least one interest in common—the topic of your speech. Think about how you can meet their needs, give them a gift, and make it enjoyable for them to hear you—even in a courtroom.

10. **Practice constructive self-talk**—Use positive coping statements that (1) accentuate your assets, not your liabilities; (2) encourage you to relax; and (3) emphasize a realistic rather than catastrophic assessment of your situation before, during, and after your speech.

11. **Be attuned to your audience, but don't misread them**—In all audiences, it is inevitable that some people will fidget, look away, walk outside (to take a call, go to the bathroom), whisper to each other, have a home or work crisis on their mind, etc. There will be silences when you pause. Expect that. While you do need to pay attention to your audience, don't misread small cues that are nothing more than the natural outcome of having a multitude of people confined in a small space listening to one person speak. The more you speak, the more you will know the difference between this and overall audience boredom or confusion.

12. **Use the fear to your advantage**—Fear creates an adrenaline rush. Use it to communicate energy and enthusiasm about your topic.

13. **Use visual imagery to enhance presentation**—This is a skill used effectively in sports, in business, and elsewhere. Visually imagining your speech is the opposite of rehearsing it (but not a replacement!). In addition to practicing it out loud, visually imagine yourself confidently and successfully giving it. Do this when you are relaxed and know your material well. Visualize each phase/step of the speech, from getting up from your chair/table to your introduction, your speech, questions and answers, and returning to your speech. Visualize success, confidence, relaxed delivery, and a supportive/satisfied audience. This takes practice too. And it is the opposite of negative self-talk.

14. **Use relaxation techniques**—Condition your body to relax. Use exercise, relaxation imagery, breathing, and muscular relaxation— alone or combined. Engage in physical exercise about two hours before you speak. Go for a brisk walk around the block. Imagine pleasant and calm situations, such as lying in a hammock or on the beach on a warm summer day. Breathe in deeply and out slowly. Systematically tense and relax various muscle groups.

    Try this relaxation exercise: close your eyes, breathe in, focus on an area of tension as you breathe out, imagine breathing out the stress with each breath you exhale, starting with your head, face and neck, then your shoulders and arms, next your chest and lungs, then stomach, and finally your legs and feet.

15. **Realize your nervousness doesn't show**—It is a rare case when an audience can tell that a speaker is nervous. Normally those butterflies in your stomach are just not visible! Nervous habits, like pacing, shifting your weight from foot to foot, or tapping a pen, are what "leak" your feelings to your audience. Tackle these and your audience will never know how nervous you are.

Example:

When I do a one- or two-day small group presentation skills training program for a client, one of the things I do is have each person of the group present in front of the group. Then I have that person speak with me outside the room while the group is writing down constructive feedback and observations for the speaker. The very first thing I ask the speaker is, "how do you feel about your presentation?" Invariably, every single person starts by criticizing his or her own presentation and then gives some variation of "I was so nervous, I know they could tell." And you know what? When I go back in the room, I ask the group if they could tell if the speaker was nervous. Almost all of the time, with the exception of extreme circumstances of "leaking your feelings," the group couldn't tell that their colleague was nervous.

Most of us judge ourselves more harshly than anyone else does.

---

16. **Reward yourself**—When you've given a speech, reward yourself for the accomplishment. Associate it with a positive, not a negative. Don't immediately concentrate on all the things you did wrong or could have done better. Think of what you did well and improved upon from your previous speeches.
17. **Let go of mistakes**—Everyone makes mistakes, even professional speakers. Don't ruminate, but rather learn from your mistakes (keep a journal if you would really like to improve), and move on.
18. **Be confident**—The more confident you are, the less fear you will have and the better impression you will make with your audience. And if you're not confident, fake it till you are.

Five Ways to Face Your Fear

Here's a list of suggestions for how to practice speaking in some non-threatening ways that build confidence. These options are easy and fairly nonconfrontational and involve little risk to you, either professionally or personally. Give them a try:

- As I mentioned previously, **join Toastmasters** (www.toastmasters .org). Its goal is to help people of all walks of life become better speakers. The focus at Toastmasters is doing the one thing we're interested in—speaking, speaking, speaking, and getting feedback from your fellow speakers who are your audience. The organization is not set up to have instructors who teach speaking skills. Instead, it is a nonthreatening forum to practice creating and giving short presentations on a variety of topics.

  Make a commitment to spend at least six months in the group at a minimum. Find one that only meets once a month, so you don't find yourself overcommitted to weekly meetings.

  It's a very safe environment. Everyone there wants you to succeed. It is a terrific forum to practice, practice, practice, reduce your fear, and eventually become very good at public speaking.

  And while you're at it, if you want to see good (nonpolitical) speeches in action, watch a few of the international Toastmaster competition finalists on video. Their ability to tell stories and captivate their audience is fantastic—they are an inspiration to watch.
- **Perform a reading at your church/synagogue/temple**—Readings are a fine stepping stone to full-on presentations. They let you speak in front of a crowd without having to worry about remembering lines. After all, you are supposed to be reading. If you stumble over a word or two in a reading, no one cares. Everyone does it.

  And if your fear of public speaking is based on your worry that you will forget what you have to say, readings are the perfect venue for you. The words are right in front of you the whole time.

Tip:
Just because you are doing a reading does not mean you shouldn't look at your audience. You should *always* lift your eyes up off the page and try to establish eye contact even if you're reading directly from a text. People like to know you're talking *to* them, not simply in their presence.

- **Go to a public forum and ask questions**—Talk about a risk-free environment. A city hall meeting is the perfect place for you to get up on your hind legs and make some noise. Next time your city hall or condo/homeowners' association or any public entity announces that they are holding a meeting and would like to hear from constituents or members, show up and be ready to ask a question or two or make a *brief* statement during public comment time.

There are lots of advantages to these types of events. First, you will not likely know anyone in the room, so you don't have to worry about getting embarrassed or tongue-tied in front of your loved ones or business associates. Next, the emphasis is not on you. It is on the subject of your question and the person whose job it is to address your question or complaint. Finally, it can be as brief (or as long) as you choose it to be. "I live on Melrose Street and we have a lot of potholes. What can we do about that?"

- **Join a committee or volunteer for a charity**—Committee meetings and attending events at a charity (apart from also being beneficial to your community) afford you an opportunity to practice public speaking without professional risk. If you join the board of directors for a small local charity or help set up a bake sale at your school or head up a Boy Scout troop, you will very often find yourself in the position of having to ask and answer questions, present plans, or offer suggestions. Take advantage of these opportunities and talk, talk, talk.

- **Give a toast at dinner.** Next time you find yourself in a dinner setting, either at your home or at a restaurant, take a moment to raise a glass to someone in the room. If it is your host, simply thank them for a lovely evening. If you are out with friends, try a brief testimonial to friendship. The key here is *brevity*. I'm not suggesting a long, drawn-out "best-man-at-the-wedding" toast. I mean one, simple sentence: "Here's to Jim and Martha. Thanks for a terrific dinner." "To Melissa on her thirtieth birthday. Here's to thirty more!" Short, simple, risk-free, and painless.

So that's my list of suggestions on how to get started. Pick one or several, or try them all if you want to really shine. What they all have in common is the absence (or at least the minimization) of risk. If your brief presentation, question, comment, or story doesn't go particularly well at one or more of the previous events . . . who cares? You haven't embarrassed yourself in a lasting way. Your professional status isn't on the line. You haven't cost your client any money or jail time. But you did manage to take a step in the direction of recognizing and owning your fear. That's a step worth taking.

Freedom to Fail

So having talked about the nature of fear, its origins, and a lot of ideas on how to fight it, you would think we had exhausted the topic, right? Wrong. There's still one last point to make. The fact is that in spite of good efforts, there will be some talks that just don't go well. That's the thing that many of us are really the most afraid of, isn't it? But maybe we should look at it from a different point of view and realize that even those failures can have value.

We know that failure has gotten a bad rap.

After all, failure is supposed to be terrible, right? If you fail, it means you didn't succeed, and if you didn't succeed, then you're awful and should probably go to jail, lose your driver's license, and be labeled an outcast. Isn't that the general idea?

There's only one problem with this scenario: Failure is *wonderful*.

There is no better teaching tool in the world than failure. Failure is the only thing that lets you know what success is really like. If you only did well, you wouldn't have anything with which to contrast it.

The world is full of examples of how terrific and universal failure truly is. After all, the best baseball players in the world fail two out of every three times they step up to the plate. Actors audition for hundreds of roles and are considered wildly successful if they get hired to do a handful of them. Scientists perform experiment after experiment, returning to the laboratory again and again, facing failure after failure. Why? Because it is through failure that you learn what to do and, maybe even more importantly, what *not* to do.

Of course, failure doesn't feel very good. Nobody likes to fail. Success is much more fun. But in order to succeed in any real way, there has to be at least the risk of failure. And any time there is a risk of something, there's a chance of that risk not paying off. The result?

Wonderful, glorious failure.

You need to dare to fail. You need to *celebrate* your failure. If you fail, *fail spectacularly*. Learn how to survive your failure and move on. Don't let it haunt you; let it teach you.

Failure is a lot like being unpopular in high school. It can be awful while you're experiencing it, but once you get past it and move on with your life, you see how unimportant it really was in the grand scheme of things. Why dwell on it?

Another thing to consider: *Everybody* fails. Olympic athletes lose races. Babe Ruth struck out far more times than he got on base. What makes a champion is the ability to shrug off these failures and concentrate on the ultimate goal, whether it is winning that gold medal, throwing that perfect game, or smacking that grand slam. Rehashing and reliving your failures gets you nowhere.

Welcome your failure, learn from it, and then toss it aside.

As philosopher William Whewell said, "Every failure is a step to success."

CHAPTER NINE

Addressing New Technology

These days, speakers have a lot of help. From software programs to videoconferencing to online venues, the world of the presenter has changed dramatically. But make no mistake, even low-tech realities like the humble printed handout require a little strategy, if you don't want to end up losing an audience's attention. For that reason, I'm going to talk in this chapter about not only how and when to distribute handouts, but how to best present yourself on teleconferences and webinars. But first, I have to lead off with—and spend a lot of time on—a software program that is often billed as The Visual Aid You Can't Live Without. But that's not what I call it. I usually call it . . .

PowerPoint—The Devil's Software Program

Let's make something clear: PowerPoint is evil.

This may strike you as being an overstatement. PowerPoint is *evil?* Seriously?

Seriously. PowerPoint truly sucks. It has single-handedly ruined hundreds of thousands of presentations, if not millions, and has corrupted just as many otherwise intelligent speakers.

My advice? Don't use it. [1] Or at least don't use it every single time you speak.

Why is this software so insidious? Why should it be avoided like a fresh outbreak of the Black Plague? Simply put, PowerPoint offers exactly the kind of crutch to public speakers upon which they should never rely. It is the public speaking equivalent of a narcotic—it feels good while you're using it, but it ultimately destroys what you are trying to achieve.

---

[1] This advice does not apply to closing arguments. See Chapter Fourteen for more information.

PowerPoint is designed to be a speaker's helper. It is supposed to frame your main points in a colorful and powerful way, support your themes with both images and memorable quotes, and generally serve as an instructive helper. PowerPoint is supposed to be there when you need it and gone when it is unnecessary.

But what PowerPoint has turned into, through overuse, misuse, and downright abuse, is the functional equivalent of a heckler. For the majority of presentations that employ it, PowerPoint does not assist the speaker in his or her task. Instead, it undercuts what would otherwise have been a coherent, thoughtful, and successful speech.

Speeches that at one time would have been fifteen minutes long, easy to follow, and informative are now thirty to fifty minutes long, contain fifty PowerPoint slides, and are really boring. Rather than providing the audience with a handy set of guideposts to aid them in their journey through the presentation, PowerPoint users instead assault their audience's senses with hundreds of unnecessary headings, bullet points, and dense paragraphs of text that do nothing to bring the speech to life.

All of which goes to say: PowerPoint is evil. You have been warned. Stay away.

Example:

In case you think I'm exaggerating about how much of a turnoff a bad PowerPoint presentation can be, let me offer as evidence the following live tweets by audience members at just such an occasion. These were collected during a keynote address at a Higher Education & Social Media conference. The keynote speaker had made just about every mistake with his slides that a person could make—too much information, bad design choices, too many slides, etc., etc. And members of the audience tweeted each other and other conference members the following not-so-subtle critiques (and these are only a sample of the tweets):

- "Clearly I'm not the only one who sucks at PowerPoint. I was smart enough not to use it though."
- "Gold font on gray background w/ 1990 drop shadow makes babies cry. Should we stage an intervention?"
- "Worst designed PowerPoint ever. Ever."
- "I think I'm about to have a seizure."
- "Why is this guy here?"
- "Okay, slides with paragraphs of information make me turn around and tweet about how such things are bad."

- "Watching people try to figure out how they can get out . . . starting to see the 'OMG, I AM TRAPPED' looks on faces."
- "I have no idea what's going on right now."
- "Someone needs a class on PowerPoint . . . Sound levels on videos . . . And being relevant to your audience."

Wow. Pretty brutal, huh?

The only difference between that audience and the audience you face is that yours is less likely to live-tweet about your presentation and more likely to criticize it to each other, or to others back at their firm, courthouse, or client office. Or they could just save it up and blog about it. Those are the risks you run with a bad PowerPoint presentation—it's not just a little bit distracting; it's downright obnoxious. Think about it.

PowerPoint, Part II: I Can't Quit You

Okay, I know that not everyone or even a majority of people are going to take my advice and ditch PowerPoint. Some people are even *required* to use it by superiors who don't know any better. It is too ubiquitous in our lives as presenters to simply toss it on the ash heap and forget about it entirely. And, in all honesty, it *can* be effectively used. In other words, "evil" in this case is relative.

Plus, I understand that despite the growing backlash against PowerPoint (and my personal abhorrence of the thing), there will be plenty of people out there who insist on using it. Maybe you'll use it because you disagree with me and think it is the best thing since sliced bread (everyone is entitled to his or her opinion). Maybe you'll use it out of habit or because the conference organizer requires it. Maybe you're using it because everyone else on the panel is employing a PowerPoint presentation and you don't want to be the odd one out.

Or maybe, just maybe, you're using it because you have some fantastic graphics to present and a great visual story you have prepared for your opening statement or closing argument. I will admit—such incidents do exist.

Whatever the reason, this chapter is dedicated to helping you use PowerPoint (or whatever slide software you like) effectively so you don't bore your audience to death. So here goes.

What Are Visual Aids For?

The primary concept you have to remember about slide presentations is that they are "visual aids." Key word being "aid." Slide decks are not, and never should be, your entire presentation. The function of these slides is to *enhance* your presentation, not to become a substitute for your presentation.

Side Story:

An example of what I am talking about occurred a few years back when I was giving several presentations at an annual ABA convention in New York. One of the IP-related committees asked me to do a short IP skills-focused program and, at the end of the presentation, we included about thirty minutes of individual coaching in front of the group. In advance of the program, the committee solicited volunteers who would speak for about three minutes in front of the crowd, after which I would critique the brave volunteers and provide speaking advice right then and there.

After we gathered about five or six volunteers, I asked all of them to send me their presentation outlines about two weeks in advance. Every single one of the volunteers sent me a PowerPoint slide deck, not a speech outline. The results, as you can imagine, were predictably awful.

As I have described in earlier chapters, always remember to create your presentation in an outline format first. Organize your main points, get them in what you consider to be the most logical order, and then begin practicing. Get your presentation *down*. Create it, practice it, modify it, cut it down, and get it as close to a final outline as you can get (see Chapter Three, Step 5: "Create Your Outlines").

When you feel that your presentation is as close to perfect as it can be, *then* you can decide what visual aids will enhance your message. Do not, under any circumstances, use PowerPoint as your word processing program. The outline belongs in a Word document or on paper, or in any other document format. *Don't even turn on the PowerPoint program until after your outline is nearly complete.* In other words, do *not* attempt to build your PowerPoint presentation as you create the speech itself. That way lies madness.

You can, as you are writing your presentation outline, add reminder notes here and there about ideas for visuals that will help you communicate your message with more impact down the road. But creating your visual aids before your speech is completed is putting the cart before the horse. The visual aids are supposed to enhance your message, not the other way around.

So what makes a good visual aid? As you can probably guess, not paragraphs full of text, super long quotes, statutes, legal opinions, or bullet point after bullet point of your speaking outline. What you want to think about using are the following:

- Photos
- Cartoons (you can have them custom made—see the "resources" appendix for people I know who will do this for you for a fee)
- Video clips, like great depo testimony (keep them short)
- Graphics, charts, diagrams (keep them *simple* and easy to skim)
- One dramatic startling statistic or phrase that will grab people's attention.

If you live by the rule that PowerPoint is a visual aid, and *not* your presentation itself, you can be creative about what types of slides you want to use to communicate your message.

Remember: PowerPoint should be used to focus attention, not diffuse it. It should provide visual and/or audio reinforcement of your message. Some people use slides just because they're used to doing it, or because everyone else is doing it or because they've gotten used to it as a kind of crutch, but those aren't really very good reasons. If PowerPoint slides will *help* you—to grab attention, to accomplish something visually, to explain something more succinctly and accurately—then go for it. Otherwise, you should seriously rethink a dependence on PowerPoint slides.

Best Tips for PowerPoint Use and Delivery

- Number one rule: Do not, and I mean *do not,* deliver your presentation directly to the screen! If you were having a conversation with a friend over coffee or dinner, would you want to be looking at the back of his or her head? No, of course not. Neither does your audience. Turning and delivering your presentation to the screen is a horrible habit in which far too many speakers indulge. Train yourself not to do it. Remember, your audience is your focus, not the screen.
- Of course, if you follow my advice and work from a speaker's outline instead of using your slides as a substitute, you shouldn't have any problem following this rule. If, God forbid, you are still using your slides as your speech outline, then at least use your laptop for your notes while you talk and not the eight-foot screen behind you. After all, it's not like you're using the old-fashioned film slides and you

have to look at the screen to make sure they are right side up! Your laptop shows you exactly which slide is on the screen.

- Avoid having too many slides. You cannot effectively use fifty to sixty slides in a one-hour presentation, much less ninety or a hundred . . . which I have seen attempted! Think about it. If you have sixty slides for a one-hour presentation, you need to discuss one slide per minute. No one can do that well. No one.

- When using slides, always allow your audience the time it takes to absorb the impact of what is on the slide—especially when you have great visuals. If you don't have this luxury, then you need to cut down the number of slides you are using. The correct solution is never to rush through your slides so fast that your audience gets irritated with you. Either take your time or don't bother.

- "Blank" your screen or use empty slides when you are *not* talking about what is on the screen. I recommend learning how to "blank" your screen using a toggle (press on/press off) switch on your computer. Usually it is Control F5, but it depends on the laptop—ask your IT person or read your manual.

  It is important to blank the screen (or use blank slides at key locations) when you have moved on to a new topic because talking about one concept while another concept is up on the screen is distracting for your audience.

- Think about screen placement. Talk to the event organizers prior to your presentation and make sure the screen is off to the side and is not the center of attention. This may sound counterintuitive, but the simple truth is that the audience is there to hear *you* speak. You, in turn, are there to talk with them. Therefore, you should be at the center of attention. The last thing you need is a six- to eight-foot screen in the front of the room, dominating the space, while you are pushed off to the side. But you see this configuration all the time.

Since most times speakers are on a platform, that platform should be front and center. *Always* have the screen in the corner (depending on the size of the room) or to the side of your platform or podium with a good amount of space between them. You also want to be sure there is enough space between the podium and/or platform and the screen that you can move out from behind the podium yourself if possible, as discussed earlier. Whether on a platform, using a podium, or just walking around with a microphone, you want to command the focal point of the room yourself.

Creating PowerPoint Slides That Don't Suck

Here are some general tips about how to avoid the pitfalls of bad PowerPoint slides:

Colors and Fonts
- Use colors that go well together and are harmonious.
- Avoid using yellow and red colored letters on white or light backgrounds.
- Avoid using black type on a dark blue background.
- Size matters. Sizing your type at 14-18 point is not large enough . . . your text needs to be 26-32 point to be readable, unless everyone is sitting in the first row. It is very frustrating for an audience member to be offered slides that are too small to read.
- Stick to one typeface or, at the most, two. Too many fonts are distracting and annoying to your audience.
- Use **boldface** and *italics* sparingly and avoid <u>underline</u>—it is hard to see these words when they are projected. The same goes for ALL CAPS.

I believe this next slide will amaze you with its avant-garde typefaces, trendy color choices, and daring use of clip art.

Using Bullet Points

- If you are going to use bullet points, try not to have more than three on any slide, but preferably only one combined with a great graphic.
- I usually tell people to use what I call the "3x5 Rule": No more than three points per slide / five words per point. Frankly, I wouldn't use more than one sentence per slide and would combine the brief text with a cartoon, photo, or other nifty graphic. Unfortunately, some people are incurable bullet point users.
- Remember, there is no need to put your main speaking points up on a screen at all. Your audience *will* understand and comprehend your theme without your having to serve it up to them on a platter.
- For two excellent resources, with examples, that will help you improve your PowerPoint slides immeasurably, check out the website "Presentation Zen" by Garr Reynolds or the book *slide:ology: The Art and Science of Creating Great Presentations* by Nancy Duarte. "Presentation Zen" has some exceptional examples of stunning, moving slides that convey a visual message simply and with impact.

More Tips about Formatting Your Text

- Keep everything on each slide simple, clear, and understandable.
- Avoid busy slides and busy backgrounds. This means you can't use a lot of the slide templates provided by PowerPoint—they're just ridiculously busy. Rule of thumb: If you have to ask yourself if the slide is too busy, the answer is yes. It is.
- Avoid putting too much information on any one slide. In fact, some of the most powerful slides I have seen have had only one point or a single word on them.
- Always remember to put your contact information on the last slide if the slides will be handed out. This is a missed marketing opportunity if you forget to do it. The only exception to this rule is when you are using slides in a courtroom.
- If you want or need your logo on your slides, just put it on the first and/or last slide. You don't need it on every slide; it just adds clutter.

Using Graphics

- As with your text, keep all of your graphics simple and easy to read. Use pictures or images that need little or no explanation. There is nothing worse than watching a speaker try to teach from, or explain, a complicated graphic with a ton of points, lines, or bars on it. If your audience needs detailed information for later use, include a hard-copy version of detailed graphs that they can take away and absorb at their leisure.

- Get the best images you can. There are copyright-free images all over the internet.
  - For free: Type your best guess at an image description into a Google search window and cull through, but be careful of violating copyrights.
  - For purchase: There are also stock photography and stock art sites online—istock and Getty Images are two popular ones—that have a huge selection for you to peruse. On the rare occasion I use PowerPoint, I may spend $1 to $2 per image, and end up paying $15 more for my presentation, but that's less than the price of a good lunch . . . definitely worth the investment.
- Don't forget that you can take your own pictures.
- Keep all of your slides readable and comprehensible. To test the effectiveness of your slides, show them to your kids or non-attorneys in advance. And when you get feedback on your slides, *listen to it.* If your feedback suggests that you need to go back to the drawing board, don't hesitate to abandon anything that is not effective.
- Make sure your graphics are of good quality. I have seen countless presentations using downloaded photos, pictures of forms or statutes, or other types of graphics, that are of poor, blurry quality. It reflects badly on you as a speaker to offer shoddy graphics to your audience. Take the time to find and present the good stuff, clean up what you have, or don't offer it up at all.
- It may sound time-consuming to go hunt up the best visuals for your slides . . . and it is. For a one-hour webinar—I only use Power-Point in webinars and only because I have to in that setting—it usually takes me three to five hours to find the right visuals to accent my points. It takes an extra commitment of time, but it pays off in the end.

Side Story:

A law professor I know tells me she almost always uses visuals in her PowerPoint presentations in class. As she says, "I may not always find the right ones when I google for images, but I am amazed at the selections—loads of tax terms have images—mortgage, debt, capital gains, etc. It is surprising what fair-use options there are out there."

Final Preparation

- Always be sure to test your slides—all of them—as soon as you get your A/V materials ready. You can do this by projecting the slides in a large room onto a screen or the wall. Check to see if the colors work, if the type is legible or too small, if your slides are too cluttered, etc.
- Practice using your visual aid prior to giving your presentation. This is especially critical if you are going to use it in a courtroom. This will help make your presentation smooth and polished and will help you to work out the kinks.
- Make sure you work with your slides, and finalize them, at *least* a week in advance. You want to give yourself time to make any adjustments necessary. Last-minute changes can be difficult and, at times, expensive.

Making Sure You Actually Get to Use Your PowerPoint

This next bit is so important it warrants its own section.

If you are not using your own laptop, always make sure you give your slide deck to the organizers by the deadline they have given. It is incredibly unprofessional to email a slide deck to the organizers the night before a presentation or, *worse*, to show up at the event (or your staff, committee, or client meeting) and hand a flash drive to the on-site person and expect him or her to make it all work perfectly for you.

I have spoken with many event organizers—corporate, CLE, in-house departments, and the like—and they all say the same thing: they do not understand why presenters think that showing up the day of the event or meeting with a flash drive is somehow acceptable or even how they can believe its use is logistically possible at that point.

Doing so is almost guaranteed to throw off the flow, timing, and organization of the meeting or program session, assuming the flash drive can be used at all.

If you do this, you take a big risk. What if there is no one at the event who can upload your slideshow from your flash drive or get it into the seminar deck the night before? What if program organizers won't allow it because it disrupts the flow and organization and makes everyone start late? What if there simply is no opportunity to upload it? What if the person after you doesn't know how to switch back into the main program deck after you are done if you don't remember to close yours, and then that speaker is left struggling to find a way to get back to his or her own slides?

What if you have links or video embedded in your presentation, but they don't work in the version of the software that the program organizer uses?

At least three or four times a year, we'll have a speaker show up at our CLE programs five minutes before he or she is set to speak and surprise us with a flash drive of a PowerPoint, or worse, links to Presi (an online slide program), YouTube, or other online video they want to use during their presentation. Sometimes it's a double whammy—a PowerPoint presentation with what they think are video links inside their slides or a bunch of separate video files on the flash drive in addition to the PowerPoint presentation.

There is nothing worse—for us and for attendees. For any program organizer, it is a logistical nightmare. They look unprepared and disorganized, and it's the company or association's reputation that is harmed, not the speaker's. Attendees always blame this on the organizer.

And most importantly for the attendees—it's unbelievably annoying to have their time wasted while they sit there for the first five or ten minutes as the organizers scramble to get the presentation up and working.

It is *definitely* not a great way to make a strong first impression.

But what, you say, could possibly go wrong? All you have to do is insert the flash drive and ask PowerPoint to access your file, right? Well, it depends. If the organizer already has a PowerPoint deck loaded for the entire day, they have to exit it to start yours, and in the meantime the entire audience gets to enjoy the desktop pictures on the laptop and the slide thumbnails before the "slide show view" is started. And then they get to enjoy it in reverse once you're finished with your presentation and the organizer has to go back to the main program deck. And that's assuming your organizer—or anyone conversant with PowerPoint and that type of laptop—is around to help and not occupied elsewhere. This usually not only delays your presentation—it delays the next one as well. There is a *reason* organizers want everything in advance.

What else? Well, these days you can have a computer/flash drive port conflict. For example, you can't even use a standard USB flash drive in the latest version of a Mac laptop (2017-2018). They use a USB-c drive, which is a completely different connection. So that means you're left without your deck if there isn't the correct converter around somewhere. And since you didn't warn the organizer, there probably isn't a converter around anywhere, or at least not the specific one you need.

What other type of technical issues could possibly arise? Well, in some older versions of PowerPoint video links or URLs embedded in a slide don't work. So your program organizer has to launch a browser tab, put in the link, and pray that the internet connection at the venue is strong enough to stream the video. Then if it is YouTube, the audience gets to watch an advertisement before the video plays.

And then there's the audio portion of the video—the audience can't hear the audio portion of your video straight from your laptop's speakers. The laptop, or projector, needs to be somehow connected to the amplification system in the room. This is not an easy task, and to work correctly it always has to be set up in advance. I can't tell you how many times I have watched organizers have to just hold a microphone up to the laptop in order for everyone to hear the audio, since the presenter did not warn the organizer in advance.

As you can see, it's not just unprofessional to show up at a program with a slide presentation on a flash drive, it is fraught with risk that you won't get to use it, that you will disrupt the program, that you will make it difficult for those who invited you to speak or for your staff at the meeting or the speaker who follows you, and that you yourself will appear unprepared and make a bad first impression.

So if you are going to use it, use it well, be prepared, and make sure your presentation gets to wherever it needs to be by the time it needs to be there.

Tip:

If you are using PowerPoint for an event or a meeting and emailing it to someone, be sure to email the final deck *from yourself*, not an assistant. Why? Because many organizers will search on your email address as their final fail-safe check to ensure they have all PowerPoint decks for the day/meeting. If the final deck (or only copy) goes to the organizer from an assistant's email address and not yours, it won't be found. Believe me, even my own company has made that mistake. And it's not fun to be at an event and not be able to use your PowerPoint because it isn't there.

Last Word . . .

Can't resist making this point one last time: If all of this in-depth information about PowerPoint sounds like too much work, you actually *can* consider speaking to your audience without slides. I teach my one- to six-hour in-person public speaking program fifteen to twenty times a year. I have done it for more than fifteen years, and I have *never* used PowerPoint. Not once. In all that time, no one has *ever* complained. 'Nuff said.

I think we've exhausted this topic. Let's take a break and get into something refreshingly old-fashioned by comparison—the simple printed handout. But these guys can still steal the stage away from you, which is why I think of them as . . .

Handouts from Hell

There are two critical things you need to know about handouts:

First of all: Don't pass them out *while* you're speaking. It will distract audience members, and since speakers tend to speak while passing out these materials, nobody listens well during that time. In other words, your message will be lost.

But you also don't want to pass them out *before* it's time for you to start, because your audience members will just read the materials while you are talking. (And usually faster than you can talk.) And that's no good either. Why not just hand out a newspaper and check in when they're finished reading?

So . . . what's a person to do?

Handouts should be "leave behinds." By "leave behinds" I mean just that. When you're done, leave them behind and let your audience members look them over after you've finished speaking. The purpose of this is twofold:

1. To provide your audience a resource they can take home with them; and sometimes,
2. For your own marketing purposes or so they can reach you.

The only exception to this rule is when you need your audience to review a form or other type of legal document or when you are having them perform an exercise. In these instances, if possible, have the materials on their tables prior to their arrival (upside down, so they'll ignore them). If they get curious and start to snoop, instruct them to leave them alone until you're ready. They'll happily comply.

What if you can't place these materials on the tables in advance? Have somebody distribute them *before* it is time for you to start (again, face down on the table) and tell the audience to leave them alone until you're ready. That will keep the focus where it belongs—on you and your presentation. Worst case, you can take a break or a pause during your presentation while the documents are distributed by someone. But you don't want to stand around waiting on your handouts to be passed out before you kick off your presentation—that's definitely not the way to start with an interesting attention-getter.

When you do, finally, need to discuss the handouts, tell the audience to pick them up and review them along with you. The key is to *always* tell your audience what to do and when. That will prevent discomfort and confusion—two things you never want to inflict on them.

Don't make the mistake of thinking that because you have an assistant distributing the materials that you can give out handouts in the middle of your presentation. The same distraction (switching their focus from you to the handout) will occur no matter *who* hands it out. But if you do have that worst-case scenario—a handout that has to be distributed during your presentation—there's no doubt that it's preferable to have someone else hand them out. In this rare and undesirable circumstance, the best way to limit the damage is to pause from your presentation while the assistant gets the handouts passed around. During this unfortunate interruption, engage in some light chit-chat to fill the time. Don't continue with your presentation, because no one will be listening to you. But don't leave a silence, because your audience will begin to talk amongst themselves.

Finally, *never* use a single handout for your audience to pass around themselves and review while you are speaking. What I mean by that is, it is critical that you *do not* give your audience one item (or even a few) to examine up close. The handout will sloooowly move around the room and, by the time everyone else has seen it, you'll likely be in your car on the way home.

If you need a visual aid, *use one.* This is the time that PowerPoint (or other projected image) can be used effectively. And if whatever you need them to see is too small to be seen on a PowerPoint slide, have enough copies so that everyone can look at the item simultaneously, instead of passing it around.

And, finally, all that said, there is one exception to the rule. When you're speaking at a Continuing Legal Education (CLE) program, the attendees there expect—and want—an outline of your presentation, preferably in advance. So, while it flies in the face of what I just said and all basic public speaking principles, it is the setting in which you many times do need to give a handout in advance. There is something about CLE programs that makes attendees want to have an outline to read and take notes upon during the program. In fact, attendees complain vociferously when a speaker at a CLE program doesn't give handouts to the attendees.

Keep in mind, however, that if you provide an outline and make reference to it while speaking, it is *essential* that you point to the page you are on while speaking. And be sure it is the page of the entire seminar book, not the page on your original, if your originals have been incorporated into something for the day. This is a common mistake among presenters, and it absolutely drives attendees nuts.

Webinars and Teleconferences

Unlike live presentations, where your audience has a chance to watch you in action—moving around the stage, engaging in eye contact with your jury, smiling at and cajoling your attendees—a webinar or teleconference is a nonvisual event. Your audience might see something (a handout or an on-screen demonstration), but they're not going to see *you*. And this is going to drastically change the way you make your presentation.

First, let's make sure we know what we're talking about. We all know what a teleconference is—you're on speakerphone or some other audio device. But what is a "webinar"?

If you haven't seen one, this is generally what you experience during a webinar: You are shown a presentation of some kind (think of it as an instructional video or boring PowerPoint slideshow) and you are taken through the slideshow presentation by an unseen speaker. That's your basic webinar. Okay, back to our area of focus: How do you make a successful presentation during a webinar?

Presenting a webinar or teleconference means relying entirely on your unseen, narrative presence. In this instance, *all you have is your voice*.

This means it's imperative that you employ all the tricks from Chapter Seven's discussion of "Vocal Dynamics" and also that you use the rhetorical techniques described in Chapter Five. After all, with your verbal skill as your only tool, you're going to need every voice-related and rhetorical trick in the book.

By the way, when thinking about your phone line (which most people don't) remember this: Wireless (land line or mobile) is the *worst* choice you can make for webinars and teleconferences because the audio quality is never good enough in this situation. Use a wired headset to ensure that your audio quality is first rate.

You also want to be sure that your headset comes equipped with a long cord so that it allows you to stand up and move around your office while speaking. Do *not* sit down, if possible, or at least not for the entire thing.

Why? Because if you're like most people, your voice won't project as well from a seated position. And when you're relying solely on your voice, you don't want to hinder it in any manner.

Next, sitting down dampens your activity level. You cannot be animated sitting down. Whether you know it or not, the listeners on the other end can tell when you lack energy. When you're participating in one of these activities, you need to be animated or you will bore everybody to tears.

You need energy! So stand up, move around, and keep the energy level high.

CHAPTER TEN

Getting Your Audience Involved

Q&A about Q&A

I get asked a lot of questions about questions. The most frequently asked question is, when should the speaker take questions? Should the Q&A come midway through, throughout, or at the end of a presentation?

My answer depends on two things: First, how big is your audience? And second, how much control are you comfortable exerting?

The larger the audience, the better it is to take questions toward the end or you risk getting derailed by too many questions. There is also the danger of running out of time. However, if you are practiced at controlling your audience and limiting the number of questions, you can solicit and answer questions throughout your speech, which is what attendees prefer—at least in an educational setting.

If you find yourself overwhelmed with too many questions, direct your audience. Tell them you have to move on, ask them to write their questions down and save them for later. And, if you aren't able to take all questions before you conclude, *always* tell your audience how they can reach you to ask more questions. Tell them you'll stay after to answer all questions, or if not, they can email you, they can call you—whatever is appropriate.

With smaller audiences, you can allow attendees to ask questions throughout your presentation and create a more intimate and interactive environment. Remember: a presentation is a conversation, not a performance. So give them a chance to ask you questions.

In general, audiences prefer to have their questions answered at the time they think of them, not at the end of your presentation. In fact, many times they resent being put off. So, if you can handle it, take the questions during your presentation. But if the audience is too large or you don't feel you can control the number of questions, play it safe and take questions before your conclusion.

Opening Up the Floor

There are several important tips to remember when you take a moment to open up the floor to questions. The first is: Don't forget to do it. And second, tell your audience when and how to ask questions—don't leave them hanging.

And, when you are almost finished with your presentation (or, even better, at transitional moments during your speech), it is always a good idea to check with your attendees and give them a chance to ask questions in case some point or other needs clarification. Don't assume you're being crystal clear every time you open your mouth. Chances are, they might need something reviewed or emphasized. Or else they're curious about something important that you haven't covered. Remember, you're trying to meet their needs. Many times a question comes up about something you forgot to (or weren't going to) cover. If you can do it briefly without getting off track, *answer it*. It's what they want to know about. That's assuming, of course, that the question covers material that isn't so off-topic that it's irrelevant to the rest of the audience.

So, rather than avoid Q&A, you should *embrace* it because it not only gives you the opportunity to press home your critical themes, it also allows you to connect directly with your audience, *interact* with them, and meet their needs. They want that. You should want it as well.

Attendees appreciate knowing that their feedback and concerns matter to you, so give their questions the weight they deserve.

Several things about your answers that you should try to remember:

1. **Repeat the question**—As soon as the question is asked, be sure to repeat it for everyone before answering, unless the audience is small enough that they all heard it. Very often, the person asking the question will not have a microphone and will not speak loudly enough for everyone to hear. So, the moment the attendee finishes his or her question, make sure that everyone in the room knows what topic you are about to address. And if your presentation is being recorded, it is especially important to repeat the question so it is on the recording before your answer.

2. **Answer the question you are asked**—This might sound like a ridiculous point to have to make, but I can't tell you the number of times a presenter will stray off-topic from their answer onto a completely irrelevant tangent. Do your audience (and yourself) a favor and answer the question as succinctly as you can. And then be done. No tangents.

3. **Don't be thrown off by stupid questions**—I know, I know. The old adage is supposed to be "There are no stupid questions." Well, there are. In fact, some questions can be really, really dumb. But whatever you do, don't let your audience know that you think so. Smile, nod, and do your best to give the clearest answer you can (as quickly as you can) and move on. If needed, tell the questioner to come up and chat with you at the break or at the end of the program for further clarification.

4. **Look at your entire audience when answering the question**— Not doing so is a common mistake. We're programmed to look at a person when answering his or her question. However, if you do that, you are basically cutting out the rest of your audience. So break the habit and remember to always look at your entire audience when answering a question—every time.

Also, it is extremely important not to let the Q&A completely derail your presentation. If you take a break to answer questions, answer two or three, bring the Q&A to a close, and then get back to the task at hand. Just be sure to let the audience know that they will have a chance to talk to you when you wrap everything up at the end. The easiest way to do this is to look at your watch and say, "We have a limited amount of time, so I need to move on, but I promise I'll leave time at the end for more questions and stay after as well."

It's amazing how much you can accomplish by telling your audience what to expect.

When I say "at the end," don't think that I mean when you are entirely finished speaking. Your final Q&A should *always* come immediately before your conclusion, even if you are on a panel. (See Chapter Four's "Catchy Conclusions.")

Why do this? Because you always want to finish strong, and it is virtually impossible to finish strong by saying "Any more questions?" You worked hard on your conclusion. Don't ruin it.

By the way, regarding that final Q&A, this is *not* the opportunity to go back and fill in all the stuff you forgot to say *during* the presentation. Your job is to clarify, not play fill-in-the-blank. Nobody will know you forgot to say something, and you'll only confuse the audience if you try to introduce new topics right at the end.

And don't be surprised, once you've finished your conclusion and have dismissed everyone for the day, when you find yourself in the middle of the *post Q&A Q&A*. Your shyer attendees will not be the ones to shoot up their hands during the presentation, but they will doubtless approach you privately when you're finished to clear up whatever lingering questions they might have or to get your advice. Again—as always—welcome these opportunities.

The wise presenter lingers afterwards and gives the audience members a chance to chat with him or her. Your audience will appreciate the extra attention more than you know. And it wouldn't kill you to hand out a business card or two, depending on the speaking situation.

Keeping the Floor

I've been asked about how to deal with the person who raises a hand to ask a question and then either (a) rambles, (b) pontificates or disagrees with you, or (c) asks question after question after question (at that moment or throughout the program).

It's almost inevitable. There is always one in every crowd—board meetings, CLE programs, training sessions, anywhere that a question can be asked.

So what's a person to do?

Let's take this one issue at a time. First, the person who rambles without ever getting to the point of the question. This is usually the person who feels the need to give a lot of background information to set up his or her question. You need to give the person a minute or so, maybe even two just in case he or she actually gets to the question—it depends on what is happening and how often the person has done this—and then you'll need to interrupt. Obviously, you do not want to appear impatient or rude, so smile when you do it. When the person takes a breath, interrupt and gently say some friendly variation of: "I don't mean to interrupt, but I've got a lot to cover and as usual never enough time to do so, so if you have a quick question, please let me know what it is, otherwise, why don't you just come on up at the break or after the program and we can chat about it." Your goal is to interrupt, get the person on point, or get him or her to ask you later. You can make some self-deprecating joke about the time, going over time, not enough time, etc., to lighten it.

The next issue concerns the person who doesn't really want to ask a question but instead just wants to teach the topic for you, or argue with you, or hear him- or herself speak. Your response is pretty much like the one before. As soon as this person takes a breath (and you don't need to wait too long for this if you anticipate that he or she is going to pontificate), you smile and say, "I don't mean to interrupt [name—if you have his or her name], but we need to continue and I have a limited amount of time here for our presentation and questions, so if you have a quick question, please let me know what it is, otherwise, it sounds like you have a lot to discuss, and I would really like to discuss it with you, so why don't you just come on up at the break or after the program and we can chat about it." Your goal here is to acknowledge that they might have something worthwhile to say—so you don't trigger hostility, which will give them a reason to keep interrupting you—and make them feel like you think it is important enough to talk with you at the break or after the program.

The next issue is the person who keeps asking question after question, tries to keep giving advice, teaching your topic or pontificating more than once, or asks questions that are so unique they apply only to that person, meaning the rest of the audience will be annoyed at the delay taken to answer a question (or many) that have no real interest to the rest of the audience.

And believe me—the rest of the audience *will* get annoyed. You don't want to lose your audience, so you have to address the problem quickly.

This one is actually the easiest. Either when such questioners take a breath, or when they raise their hand and before they start actually speaking, you say some version of, "I can tell you have a lot of questions on this topic" or "I can see you have a lot you want to discuss about something very specific to your interests," and then "but I have a lot to get through and a limited amount of time. I really am interested in what you have to say and want to answer your questions, so can you write them down and come up on the break or after the program so we can discuss them?" Your goal here is the same as above. You want them to feel valued and that you are not dismissing their questions or their thoughts. You want them to feel that you really will discuss it with them and/or answer their questions on the break or after the program. By asking them to write it down (in the case of questions), you are confirming for them that you are sincere about being willing to chat with them later.

Then there is the final problem. Sometimes you have the person I mention above—they like to argue, teach for you, or hear themselves speak.

Over and over again. Shy of an outright heckler, which I am not going to address in this book since they are so rare in a professional setting, this is the most difficult person to deal with when speaking.

If this is any type of professional seminar such as a CLE program, bar event, or pretty much any other public presentation setting (that is not a government agency presentation), you just have to be firmer and more insistent with the "let's talk about it during break or after the presentation," and you have to do it before such audience members open their mouth. If you can move around, walk past them so your back is to them when they are at their worst, as it's hard for them to ask you a question when you are not looking at them. If you can't move, just don't make eye contact with them. Definitely don't make eye contact with them when answering the question and never ever ask "did that answer your question?"

One final tip regarding the opposite end of the scale: If you anticipate being among a group of strangers or attendees that might not feel comfortable asking questions when prompted, it frequently works to plant a questioner of your own in the crowd to prime the pump. After that person asks a question, it may prompt others in your audience to do so. If they don't, they don't. Move on.

PART TWO

JUST FOR ATTORNEYS

In the preceding pages, you read a great deal about what you should do in a variety of settings, including the courtroom, and how you can (and should) improve your message and your image/delivery. But you don't have to take my word for it.

I have interviewed many judges and justices over the course of the past fifteen years in order to get their advice and pass that advice on to attorneys when I speak. And I can tell you—they *all* say the same thing. Some of what they say reinforces what I have already talked about in the first part of this book, and much of it expands upon those ideas and provides deeper insight.

I've compiled some of their responses in the oral argument chapter of this Part Two (see Chapter Eleven) and the trial advocacy chapter (Chapter Fifteen).

Additionally, for the appellate argument, opening statement, and closing argument chapters (Chapters Twelve, Thirteen, Fourteen, respectively), I invited a few trial and appellate attorneys, and a retired judge, to share their experience and advice. All of them are highly respected in their fields, and they are some of the most highly rated speakers at our Pincus Professional Education CLE Programs as well.

Lastly, media relations. Since the beginning of the printing press, a handful of attorneys have needed to know about crisis communication and public relations. That number increased markedly with the advent of television. But it was still a small percentage.

With the arrival of social media and most especially Twitter and YouTube, having at least some knowledge of crisis communication and public relations skills is critical for a much, much greater percentage of the legal world.

And crisis communication—saying the right thing in a public forum, to a reporter, on television, or on social media—is still a form of public communication. In fact, as you will see in the last chapter of this book, there are many communication rules that overlap between public speaking and speaking with the media.

So the topic of media relations warrants a chapter as well (Chapter Sixteen).

CHAPTER ELEVEN

Oral Argument Is a Dialogue, Not a Monologue

Eight Rules from the Bench

Rule #1: Answer the Question—and Answer the One You Are Asked

Very often during your motion or appellate argument, you will, if you are lucky, be interrupted by a judge or justice asking a question.

The number one complaint I hear from judges and justices is about attorneys who don't answer their questions.

As the late Florida Supreme Court Justice Arthur J. England put it to me:

> When the question is asked, an immediate answer followed by an explanation is what you're looking for . . . . Time and again it will count against an attorney when a judge or justice has to say to them, "You haven't answered my question." And if a judge has to do it more than once, it's not only frustrating, it's really not helpful. The answer is always, "Yes," "No," or "That's not in the record," and then the explanation follows. That's the biggest flaw I see in attorneys.

So that means the number one thing I can say to you about arguing your motions before a judge (or justice) is this:

Listen to the question.

Answer the question.

And make sure you are answering the question that was asked.

This is what you can never forget when it comes to arguing any type of motion, at the trial or appellate level. So, how do you make absolutely sure this occurs?

First, listen to the *whole* question before you start formulating your answer. One reason attorneys sometimes fail to answer the question is that they don't listen to the whole question. It is perfectly acceptable for you to take a moment to think about the question after it is asked. In fact, I have had many judges, justices, and even staff attorneys who sit in on thousands of arguments over their careers say that they respect attorneys who take a moment to think about their answer before launching into it.

Second, as Justice England said, start with yes or no and *then* launch into your explanation. If the question truly doesn't ask for yes or no, then by all means, begin with your explanation.

Third, if the answer to your question is an admission regarding something that may (or will) hurt your case, make the admission and then explain why the answer doesn't affect the outcome of your case, or why it should be ignored, or even, if a plausible argument, why the precedent governing your case that would be affected by that answer should not be followed—and possibly even new precedent should be set—and *why*. Of course at the trial level your judge is not likely to be the one to overset that precedent, but it gives you the opportunity to argue it on appeal.

Whatever you do, do not lie, do not obfuscate, and do not engage in any unethical behavior in order to avoid answering the question. This may be an obvious thing to say, but it bears repeating given the number of stories I have heard from judges, justices, and their staff attorneys over the years.

True Story:

I will never forget the time that Judge William Bauer of the Seventh Circuit told this story at one of our appellate seminars in Chicago. He said he was on a panel and an assistant state's attorney was arguing the appeal. The opposing side's position was that the state had stipulated to something (I cannot remember what). Members of the appellate panel asked the state's attorney if the state had indeed stipulated on that issue. The attorney dodged the question over and over by starting with some type of equivocation and never saying yes or no. Judge Bauer jumped in at some point when everyone was frustrated and asked the question again, but when he did so he told the attorney that the attorney could answer the question "yes" or "no" and say nothing else after that. What happened? The attorney *still* did not answer yes or no, he started again with some type of equivocation. I do not remember the outcome of the case or even the response from the judges after that, but I do remember that the story—and the name of the attorney—stuck with the Judge well after the argument had occurred. And it made enough of a lasting impression that Judge Bauer retold it often.

If you are going to disagree with a judge after he or she has asked a question or made a comment, do not under any circumstances start your sentence as follows: "With all due respect, Your Honor . . . ." It's well known that judges interpret that sentence to mean you think they are idiots. I have had many judges tell me that an attorney should, instead, simply start with "I disagree, Your Honor, because . . . ." Make sure you include the "because" and explanation that follows and that your tone and nonverbals are consistent and respectful.

Here you are not arguing with the judge—and you really don't want to do that—you are engaging in a conversation about the case and you are providing a clear, hopefully defendable, rationale as to why you disagree, or at least one that will make the judge stop and reconsider his or her position on that issue.

Additionally, when you do have the opportunity to answer a question that has been posed to you, it is important not to lose your composure. Trust that you know the material and can explain it in a cogent fashion that supports your cause. Senior United States District Court Judge Paul Huck (Florida) put it this way:

> Think about the *why* . . . . The law and the rules of evidence, procedure, are by and large very logical . . . . And if you get stuck about anything, just sit back for a second. Forget about the rules of evidence, forget about law school, and say, *what makes sense*?

Assuming you're an intelligent individual and you have some sense of your own—which I assume is the case—you're going to get the right answer. Just sit back, don't panic. What makes sense? What should I do in this situation? What's logical?

And if I could teach nothing other than that, that's what I would teach my law students. Step back and take a deep breath and say, "Okay. What makes sense?"

Simply put, you should walk into the courtroom knowing that you will likely be interrupted by the judge or justice presiding over the case and he or she will likely put a number of questions to you and you should welcome that opportunity to discuss those issues of interest to the judge.

As I say again and again at my seminar, questions are like big flags—they help you see where the judge wants and even needs additional information about a particular issue. They are opportunities to clarify the reasons the judge should find in your client's favor. Justice England again:

As an oral advocate, you *want* to be asked questions because you want to know what's on their [the judge's] mind.

Your mantra for arguing a motion?

Oral argument is a dialogue, not a monologue. Or said differently, oral argument is a conversation, not a presentation.

Rule #2: Know Your Case and Your Facts Inside and Out

Another frequent complaint I hear from judges and justices concerns attorneys—and apparently, a large *number* of attorneys—who don't know their case's facts and law well enough when arguing before the bench.

Sometimes this happens because the motions were written months before the actual hearing. Sometimes it happens because someone else—like a more junior attorney—wrote the brief. Regardless of why it happens, it trips up attorneys all the time. And it affects their credibility.

United States Magistrate Judge Edwin Torres told me of his frustration in questioning lawyers on a case who are clearly not prepared or able to answer the question in a cogent way. As he put it:

> You'd be surprised how many times the lawyer won't know the most relevant fact, nor the legal disposition. You can imagine how frustrating that is. I feel like at that point I have wasted my time. This hearing was . . . well I could have been watching TV for half an hour, for all I got done. That's the biggest pet peeve.

And I'll never forget the hearing I watched as a law clerk, after working on an administrative law case for an entire year for Federal District Court Judge Oliver W. Wanger in Fresno, California. The defense had perpetuated several glaring misstatements of the record in multiple briefs, despite complaints from the plaintiff's attorney. At the law and motion argument the defense attorney started to again misstate the record. Judge Wanger stopped her, read her the correct facts from the record, and took her to task for either not knowing her own case well enough, or possibly intentionally misstating the record.

That is the last place in which an attorney wants to find himself or herself.

There is never a good reason to walk into a courtroom without knowing the facts and law of your case. Being crazy busy is not an excuse and doesn't serve your client well.

I also frequently recommend attorneys create what I call a one-page "cheat sheet" as an easy reference guide that includes the issue, the critical case or cases, the holdings, the case citation, and a reference to the page number in the brief. Also include the procedural facts surrounding the case—the court, the judge, anything else that might be helpful if asked about by your judge. That way when it comes up, you can direct the judge easily to the correct place in the brief—looking organized and on top of things yourself.

Rule #3: Assume the Judge Has Read Your Motion (A.K.A. "Don't Read Your Motion to Me!")

Across the board, this is a pet peeve among *all* judges. Judges cannot stand to have a lawyer appear before them who does nothing more than recite the language from his or her motion, whether directly from the brief or from a written speech.

For starters, the assumption *must* be that the judge has read the brief. This is not always the case (sometimes, indeed, the judge has *not* read the brief), but making the assumption that your judge is coming into the hearing or motion completely ignorant of the facts and the issues is not a good way to kick off things.

One of the Superior Court judges in Ventura County, California, whom I interviewed, put it like this:

> One of my pet peeves has always been the attorney who, in the guise of argument, is reciting what he or she has already put in their motions. Whether it's true or not in all courts, at least in *our* court, it's better for the attorney to assume that we have read the papers. We also have a research memo from a research attorney. We really do know what the case is about, or at least what the motion is about. Most of us, I think, use the research memo as a road map. Now, I know what I'm looking for. So, the attorney that sits there and takes up the time reciting what's already on the paper rather than emphasizing a point, whatever the pertinent issues are, it does their client no service at all. And really ticks me off. *Give me something that I need to know.*

In truth, reading your motion to the judge is a sign to him or her that *you* are not prepared. If you were, you could easily address the issues and cite the facts with only a glance at your notes.

Be. Prepared.

Rule #4: Know Your Judges and Let Them Do Their Job

Judges are naturally inquisitive, so they are likely to ask you some questions during the course of an oral argument. Some lawyers take these questions as a signal that the judge either doubts your ability or has concerns about your case. While this could be true at times, it is best to assume that the judge is merely trying to clear up some points, make a clear record, or even persuade one of the other judges or justices on the bench (at an appellate argument).

Justice Arthur J. England described it this way:

> I always like a good oral argument. I liked them when I was on the bench, and I like them when I'm in front of the bench. I like what has come to be called over the years a "hot court." The justices come prepared. They know the issues. They know the record, somewhat. You know it better, but they think they know it. They've been into it. . . . And it is a mistake to presume that something is a friendly question, or even worse, to presume that it's a hostile question.

Questions are asked to probe both sides, and the good minds on a court will probe both sides or will have one area that is most important for them to make sure they understand and get it right.

So, if you treat all of them as serious questions, well-intentioned, and not from a biased perspective, you can't go wrong.

If you find yourself faced with the possibility of going before an unfamiliar judge or courtroom setting, a smart idea would be to do some reconnaissance as I mention in Chapter Two, "Audience." Go to the courtroom weeks before your hearing or trial is scheduled and watch how the judge runs his court. See what the protocol is before this jurisdiction. Befriend the bailiffs and law clerks—ask non-controversial questions about the judge: "How does the judge usually handle motion practice?" "Does he or she issue a tentative from the bench?" "Does he or she allow for argument?" "Does he or she ask a lot of questions, or not many, or none?" You may get an answer or you may not, but if you do, you will walk in more prepared.

Remember, no two judges are the same. Justice Arthur J. England said:

> It's good to know how judges ask questions. Some are curt. Some are over-deferential. Some talk too long.

If you've already seen the judges in action and know what to expect, it lessens the likelihood of your being caught off-guard or flat-footed. So—know your judge.

Rule #5: Organize Your Presentation in Advance (Based on Most of the Basic Rules of Public Speaking)

This is the point where I send you back to Chapter Three on organizing your speech. While an oral argument at the trial or appellate level is not the same as a general speech, some of the basic organization principles apply. Here are the top five things to consider:

1. You want to have only a couple of main points. Three is great, two is fine, four starts to be too many. Don't try to present every topic in your brief, though you always want to be ready to respond to something the other side or the judge brings up that is not in your outline.
2. Always start with your most important argument first. You may never get to the next ones. Pick the issues that most need an oral discussion; don't pick the stuff that you argued so well in the brief it needs no further mention. Remember, this is your one last opportunity to clarify points and arguments with your judge.
3. Use transitions between your points. Help the judge(s) follow your arguments. They are just as human as any other audience.
4. Use an outline, not a speech that is written out.
5. Be prepared to shift your presentation entirely to meet the needs of your audience, i.e., your judge, once she or he starts asking questions.

That said, there are also some things from the first part of this book that you do not want to take into the courtroom with you, when arguing at the trial or appellate level.

First, this is one of the settings where starting with an attention-getter is not the best way to go. There is protocol in a courtroom that must be followed, including stating your name and client's name for the record. After that, always state the relief you are seeking from the court. Don't force the judge or justices to interrupt you halfway through with the question, "Counsel, what exactly is it you are asking for?" Ouch. And yes, I have seen that happen.

Lead with the requested relief, and you end with the requested relief.

Second, while rhetorical techniques like similes, analogies, and metaphors can sometimes be effective in this setting, be very careful what you choose to use, if you decide to use one. You'll also want to avoid those stories designed to move and intrigue your audience. Your sources here are your facts, your case law, statutes, the record, and precedent.

And avoid overusing the repetition technique; it will frequently backfire. Judges want you to get to the point, not repeat it for effect or impact.

Rule #6: Humor Is Useful . . . and Very Dangerous

The courtroom is a risky place to try to get laughs. Judges consider and rule upon matters in all seriousness, and they expect you to conduct yourself accordingly. That said, human beings are naturally funny creatures, and humorous moments are bound to crop up in court now and again. This is completely natural and to be expected. When such a moment happens, you can take advantage of it (e.g., by using self-deprecating humor if you trip or drop your notes).

There is no single point more paradoxical to the judges and justices I interviewed than the use of humor during a trial or hearing. All of them seemed to frown upon it as a general practice . . . and then proceed to tell me a funny story about something that happened to them in court. But they all had the same message: "Do as I say, not as I do."

The judges I interviewed mainly cautioned against trying to be a "funny" lawyer. Judges do not like a cutup in their courtroom. While moments of humor may sneak their way into a proceeding, there is too much danger in looking like you are making light of the case rather than giving it your serious attention. Justice Arthur again:

> I guess the point is that humor will take the edge off something. But I would caution everybody who is new at the game never to intentionally use humor. It is very, very hard and usually unsuccessful. Members of courts do not appreciate jokes during the seriousness of argument. They do not appreciate sarcasm. They don't get jokes that you think are funny or cute. I guess if I were counseling lawyers, I would say *always* stay away from attempts at humor in the course of a presentation to a judicial body of any type.

The safest route seems to be: If humorous moments happen accidentally, welcome them and then let them pass by. But do not attempt to force anything funny into the proceedings if you can avoid it.

> **Example:**
> Honey Kessler Amado, co-author of Chapter Twelve on "Appellate Oral Argument," sent me this email when I asked for a story: "I never tell jokes at oral argument and never personalize the issues. But I do recall one particularly enjoyable moment at oral argument before the Honorable Arleigh Woods (Second District, California Court of Appeal) some 24 years ago: after stating my appearance, I began by saying that everyone measures time differently, and that I had filed my Appellant's Reply Brief immediately before giving birth to my third child and that child was now walking. (The Division had been missing one justice for at least a year, which explained some of the delay.) Everyone in the courtroom laughed, including Justice Woods; and when the laughter subsided, I said: and, Your Honor, she was slow to walk."

Rule #7: Be Clear, Be Concise, Be Seated[1]

Lengthy presentations will get you nowhere. Make your point, use the law and the facts to support your point, and be done. And if a tentative has been announced in your favor? "Thank you, your Honor, if you have no other questions, I rest." That's it.

Remember these rules of good delivery:

- Make your points briefly but accurately.
- Avoid using words like "clearly" and "obviously." As one judge put it to me, "If it was that clear or obvious, we wouldn't be sitting here today."
- Speak at a conversational pace—don't go too quickly or too slowly.
- Project your voice so the judge and court reporter can hear you.
- If you want a clear record, provide the court reporter ahead of time with a list of uncommon words, acronyms, names of people, and all case names and their citations.

Rule #8: Keep It Above Board

Judges expect disagreement in the courtroom, but as you probably know, they loathe disrespect and conflict. So don't squabble with opposing counsel. Remember who your audience is: the judge. Remember what else you

---

[1] This is my variation of Franklin D. Roosevelt's "Be sincere; be brief; be seated," which I love, so I couldn't resist.

want—a clear record. You neither meet the needs of your audience, nor create a clear record, when arguing with opposing counsel at a motion hearing.

So keep things civil and professional and do not engage if your opposing counsel attempts to do so, even if you are dying to clear up a point right then and there. If it is *absolutely* necessary to your case to clarify something, you may ask the judge for an opportunity to respond briefly to something opposing counsel stated in his or her oral argument. But don't be surprised if the judge says no.

A final note as we move forward to the next chapter on "Appellate Oral Argument." Much of Chapter Twelve, written by guest authors, can also be applied at the trial level. Some of it will sound familiar, especially the "Presenting the Argument" section, as I have already discussed it in this chapter and throughout this book. The guest authors wrote their chapter without having read this book (and vice versa). The rest of the chapter provides a treasure trove of new advice.

And all of it is worth bearing in mind every time you step up to the podium to argue your case before a judge or justice.

CHAPTER TWELVE

Appellate Oral Argument: A Purposeful Conversation

Honey Kessler Amado, Law Offices of Honey Kessler Amado;
Robin Meadow, Greines, Martin, Stein & Richland LLP; and
Benjamin G. Shatz, Manatt, Phelps & Phillips, LLP

Justice Stephen Breyer of the United States Supreme Court has described oral argument as a conversation. Its purpose is to help the court decide the case. You help the court by having a well-developed argument and by answering the court's questions.

Although oral argument is usually optional, given its purpose, it should not be waived. This is counsel's only chance to discuss the case with the justices who will decide it. (This chapter refers to all judges on the appellate level—state and federal—as justices.) Further, because appellate courts rarely provide tentative opinions before oral argument, counsel rarely knows whether the court has questions about the case or has made a factual or legal error in its analysis. Waiving oral argument means losing a critical opportunity to affect the decision. Indeed, several appellate justices have commented that they are surprised when counsel waive argument; it suggests that counsel is not interested in engaging with the court.

Preparing for Oral Argument

The key to effective oral argument and confident delivery is preparation. As one colleague says, "Become master of the record and the law." Begin with reviewing your record summaries, and go back into the record itself to confirm critical factual points. Then read all the briefs. If a brief contains a factual statement that you do not recall from your review of the record, go back to the record to be certain the statements are correct or appropriately complete or contextualized.

As you review the record and briefs, begin reviewing the law. Re-read the statutes and leading cases on which you and your opposition rely. As time has passed between briefing and preparing for oral argument, a re-reading of the key cases is warranted, and the fresh reading may bring different insights about them. Research whether there have been any changes to the controlling statutes or any new decisions that may affect the case. If there are a number of relevant or key cases, you may find it helpful to create a chart or other summary of the cases—including citation, key facts, and holding—for easy reference during argument.

If there is a new, significant case on point to your factual or legal issues, bring that case to the court's attention. (See your state and local procedures for doing so.) If your preparation reveals a critical case that you did not discuss in your brief in advance or that is necessary to respond to appellant's reply brief, send a letter to the court, copied to opposing counsel, stating that you will refer to the case at oral argument.

When preparing, think anew about the case. Consider the strengths of your opposition: what is his or her best argument? Consider the weaknesses of your case: where is it vulnerable? Consider whether there are policy issues that you should address or that the court may raise. Anticipate the questions of the court. And ask yourself whether you can succinctly say where the trial court erred and why—or why its decision was correct—under the governing standard of review and controlling law.

Corral your thoughts into organized notes. The notes should address all of the points that you want to make. Your argument should be focused on a few main points, not necessarily on every issue raised in your brief. But be prepared to answer questions on any points raised in your brief. The notes should include a carefully prepared opening that summarizes your position, capturing the justice and reason of your side of the case.

Organize all your materials for oral argument into a notebook. The notebook—which for preparation purposes can be physical or digital (for example, using Microsoft's OneNote)—should include your argument notes, copies of relevant statutes, summaries or copies of relevant cases, your chart of cases, a timeline of critical events, a list of essential facts, and key documents from the record that you may need to reference during argument. Whether you take the notebook to the lectern is a matter of personal style. Some lawyers prefer having just a page of notes, and some take no notes at all to the lectern.

The final step of preparation is practice. Say your argument aloud. Stand in your office, with your notebook, and give your argument to nobody in particular! Video it and review the recording. How does it sound to your ear? Does hearing it expose weaknesses, inconsistencies, flawed logic, or awkward transitions? Does it evoke questions? Work on these questions or weaknesses. After this polishing, practice it again. And again. Become so familiar with the arguments—familiar, not memorized—that you can easily access parts of the argument when answering the court's questions.

When you can assemble a moot court, do so. But do not be discouraged if moot court is not available. You can still practice, polish, practice, and practice again ("the Four P's")!

Presenting the Argument

Be sure you know how much time you have to present. In the California state appellate courts, each party is generally allowed to designate how much time it wants for argument, up to a maximum of thirty minutes. The calendar notice will most likely disclose any different practice. In the federal appellate courts, the court will decide how much time is allocated to each side, also up to thirty minutes each side. Again, check the state, federal, and local rules.

- **Do not give a prepared speech**—Oral argument is not a closing argument, and an impassioned speech will not persuade—or even impress—the court. The conversation is the persuasion.
- **Your notes and outline are your guide for the conversation, not your script**—If you have a "cold bench" that does not ask any questions, your notes will be the logical sequence of your argument. If you have a "hot bench" that interrupts with questions, depart from your sequence but use the information in your notes to answer the questions. Questions are your friends. Questions allow you to focus on what interests the court. They provide insights into what concerns the court and can reveal a critical misunderstanding of the facts.
- **Listen to the questions**—Ask the court to repeat a question if you are not sure of it (or, as happens, cannot hear it). If necessary, take a moment to think about the question. A justice may not be arguing or rejecting your point; he or she may simply be seeking help on how to write up a point. Sometimes a justice poses a question in an effort to resolve a debate among the justices or lobs a "softball" designed to underscore a point to another member of the panel.
- **Answer the questions, and answer them immediately**—This is imperative—never just say that you will return to the point. If

the court has a question, that is all that interests the court at that moment. If you are asked a "yes" or "no" question, answer with a direct "yes" or "no" and then explain your answer. If the court asks a hypothetical, answer it. Sometimes the court is exploring concepts through hypotheticals. After answering, if necessary, distinguish the hypothetical from your case or bring the court back to your facts. Concede weak points; it preserves your credibility. But explain why that weak point is not controlling or fatal. If you are uncertain of an answer, state that. Where appropriate, explain why you are uncertain. If the point is critical, ask for an opportunity to submit a short letter brief on the question. If the court thinks the answer is critical, it will probably give you that opportunity.

- **Listen to your opponent's argument**—What has the court asked counsel? Do the questions reveal that the justices—or some of the justices—agree with you? Where is the court struggling? As respondent, start with these points. Clarify a point that your opposition could not; clarify any misunderstanding or misstatements about the record. Help resolve the court's struggle. If the questions indicate that the court is sympathetic to your argument, reinforce the point by citing to the record or relevant authorities to assure the court that its sympathies are well-founded.

Know when to sit down. If it is clear that the court has fully accepted your argument, as reflected in the questions to your opponent, you should offer to submit on that issue "unless the court has any questions."

Side Story:

Some years ago, in an appearance before Division One of the Second District (California Court of Appeal), as I came to the podium for my argument, the Honorable Ruben Ortega got up to leave the bench, saying that he was not on our panel. I said, "I am sorry Your Honor is leaving as it is always a pleasure to argue to you." He decided to stay, and I said that since he was not on my panel, if he thought I was missing anything, he should feel free to mention it. When my excellent and pleasant opposing counsel got up to argue, she said, "Your Honors, it is always a pleasure to argue to all of you!" Hers was a perfect response to my comment, and everyone in the courtroom, including me, laughed.—Honey Amado

When the court has completed asking its questions and you have covered all your points, **argument is finished.** Try to end on a strong note, ideally with a prepared closing that summarizes why you should win or what relief you want (e.g., a full reversal, or reversal and remand on particular issues). Some counsel end with the prepared closing alone; others will then ask if there are any further questions as a final deference to the court. The final courtesy is to thank the court for its attention.

It is often said that we give three arguments—one we prepare to give, one we actually give, and one we give on the way home. The one on the way home is always the best. But when well prepared, the one we actually give can be very satisfying, whatever the outcome.

Honey Kessler Amado is an Appellate Law Specialist, certified by the State Bar of California Board of Legal Specialization. She is AV-rated by Martindale-Hubbell, and is listed as a Southern California Super Lawyer. She is a frequent lecturer and writer in the areas of appellate law and family law. In 2012, she was a visiting, adjunct professor in family law and lecturer on legal writing at the University of Osijek, Faculty of Law, in Osijek, Croatia. She may be contacted at amado@ amadolaw.com.

Robin Meadow is a partner at Greines, Martin, Stein & Richland LLP, which limits its practice to appellate law. He is a frequent writer and speaker on appellate law and has pioneered electronic briefing in California's appellate courts and the Ninth Circuit. He is listed among the top 100 Southern California Super Lawyers and in Best Lawyers in America in Appellate Law, and is ranked in Band 1 for appellate law by Chambers and Partners. He received a California Lawyer of the Year award in 2016, and the Pamela E. Dunn Appellate Justice Award from the Los Angeles County Bar Association in 2014. He may be contacted at rmeadow@gmsr.com.

Benjamin G. Shatz, a partner at Manatt, Phelps & Phillips, LLP, is an Appellate Law Specialist, certified by the State Bar of California Board of Legal Specialization. He is AV-rated by Martindale-Hubbell and is listed in Super Lawyers and Best Lawyers. He is a frequent lecturer and author on appellate practice. He may be contacted at BShatz@manatt.com.

CHAPTER THIRTEEN

Opening Statements

Karen Kimmey, Farella Braun + Martel

The opening statement is the attorney's first opportunity to tell the jury what the case is about and what the attorney expects the testimony and evidence will show. It is also counsel's first real opportunity to establish his or her themes and build rapport with the jury. In order for an opening statement to be effective, it is critical that the attorney has carefully prepared, planned, developed, and practiced the opening statement. The attorney should discuss his or her theory of the case. The statement should include all of the uncontested facts as well as the client's version of the disputed facts. It should be non-argumentative, logical, simple to comprehend, and believable. In short, the opening statement is storytelling.

Opening Statement Theme

Every opening statement should have a theme. The theme shared in the opening statement should be revisited throughout the case and should be reinforced by the evidence. As a result, it is critical that the attorney is well prepared and has an intimate understanding of the facts, deposition testimony, witnesses, evidence, strengths, weaknesses, and jury instructions. This intimate understanding of the complete case will help the attorney develop the theme that will assist the jury in remembering and understanding the case from the client's perspective.

Ideally, the theme will be one that resonates with jurors and is consistent with their existing views on how people act and what motivates behavior. The theme should be relatable and not legalistic. For example, a theme like "This is a case about a defendant who made a promise, but then regretted it and is now trying to get out of the deal he made" is more effective than

"This is a case about whether two parties formed a valid contract." Even the most complex or technical case should tell a human story.

Opening Statement Strategy

In order to deliver a case-winning opening statement, the attorney should be efficient, non-argumentative, trustworthy, persuasive, and strategic.

As far as efficiency, jurors are often anxious to hear from the witnesses and receive evidence. In complex cases, the jurors may have been sitting around for days listening to the lawyers dig into their personal history and potential biases. Candidly, by the time the jury is sworn in, they are tired of hearing from the attorneys and prefer to see and hear something else. As such, it is critical for the attorney to make good use of his or her time by providing the jury with a concise story of what occurred and what the evidence will show. Counsel should aim to present the opening statement in as little time as he or she realistically can. Rarely is it advisable to use all of the time permitted by the court for opening.

The opening statement is not argument. An argumentative opening statement will likely draw a sustained objection from opposing counsel, frustrate the presiding judge, and cause the attorney to become distracted or flustered. It is also important that the attorney does not oversell the evidence or testimony. If the attorney is unable to deliver on the oversold evidence or testimony, opposing counsel will remind the jury at closing. It is best to under-sell and over-deliver. Of course, the opening statement is also not merely a neutral recitation of facts—it should persuade through a clear and strategic recitation of the facts, not through argumentative rhetoric.

Counsel should anticipate the weaknesses in the client's case and, if the weakness is admissible, volunteer the information to the jury. It is important that the jury believes the attorney is credible and honest. Attempting to hide the weaknesses or the damaging facts may cause the jury to think that the attorney and the client are attempting to pull a fast one.

Before presenting an opening statement to the jury, counsel should review the opening with colleagues and others with little or no familiarity with the case. If the case is not sufficiently large to justify a formal mock trial or retention of a jury consultant, then family members, friends, and law firm staff can be excellent sounding boards! Obtain feedback on the proposed theme. Push for honest reactions; explore the listeners' questions and evaluate the effectiveness of the approach.

> **Example:**
> Nothing is worse than over-promising and under-delivering. In one case I tried, opposing counsel repeatedly talked about how "every witness will tell you that his client took a particular step." In fact, the evidence ended up being far murkier. In closing, I was able to blow up opposing counsel's statement from opening, and follow it with bullet points of testimony from witnesses who contradicted counsel's assertion. I reminded the jury that counsel had not delivered what he had promised. Do not make categorical statements to the jury about particular evidence unless you are sure such evidence will be presented.

Anatomy of an Opening Statement

As mentioned above, the anatomy of an opening statement is similar to telling a story. The difference is that the opening statement is designed to be persuasive, while not crossing the line into argument.

Every good opening statement begins with an introduction that is catchy and memorable. The first few lines of the opening statement are going to set the tone for the rest of the opening statement. They should spark the jurors' curiosity and give them a reason to listen to what comes next. The introduction will also set out the primary theme.

There is no single way to organize the body of an opening statement. Perhaps the most common approach is to discuss the relevant facts chronologically. Particularly if the sequence of events or dates are important, timelines can be invaluable in an opening statement. In other cases, however, it may be more useful to organize the presentation around the individual witnesses who will testify, with a discussion of what their testimony is expected to establish (again keeping in mind the caution to not promise any testimony that might not be delivered). A final approach is to organize the statement thematically, addressing the various components of the case and the evidence that relates to those components. (For example, if the case involves allegations of separate but related acts of misconduct, the opening statement might address each of those alleged acts as a separate topic, regardless of how they relate to each other chronologically.)

The key, however, is to ensure that the opening has a clear, organizational structure. If jurors feel that counsel is rambling, they are likely to tune out. Jurors will pay more attention if they can understand why what the lawyer is saying is important, and if they see how each fact fits into the overall presentation. If the opening statement is going to be more than a few minutes long, it is useful to provide jurors with a roadmap up front of the topics to be covered (ideally no more than three to four bullet points). This can help them place the information they are hearing into categories that allow them to better process and retain the information, and to put it together in a way that fits into the client's theory.

Use language that is simple and declarative, without being condescending. Avoid legalese. Most experts recommend the use of the present tense when recounting the relevant events. This technique can create a more engaging story and a greater sense of immediacy.

Counsel should not feel compelled to discuss every piece of helpful evidence in the opening statement or to address every point anticipated from the opponent. Instead, he or she should focus on the most essential facts—the heart of the case—and leave the jury curious to learn more. It is unlikely that jurors, who are hearing about the case for the first time, will be able to retain more than a handful of key points; the points made in opening should be the ones that are most important to the case. Repetition is also essential to drive home the key facts and themes.

Every opening statement should have a conclusion that is as strong and compelling as the introduction. The theme that was established at the outset should be restated. The conclusion should leave jurors with a desire to take action based on the information provided.

Delivery

Jurors often are quick to form opinions regarding the competence and credibility of counsel. Aside from voir dire (which is severely limited in many courts), opening statement is counsel's first chance to make an impression on the jury. Jurors appreciate counsel who are efficient and respectful of their time, well prepared, credible, and easy to understand.

How does a lawyer create such an impression with a jury? Aside from being well prepared and knowing the evidence, a lawyer's delivery style and nonverbal behaviors will have a substantial impact. Every lawyer must determine the delivery style that is most true to himself or herself. A lawyer who is naturally reserved will look false if he or she puts on a flashy demeanor before the jury. A lawyer must work to maintain the jury's interest, but too much drama or too many gimmicks in an opening are likely to fall flat, and potentially draw an objection. Speak clearly and with conviction—aim for the style of a trusted educator.

While notes are helpful to ensure that all important points are covered, counsel should never merely read from notes. Practice the opening statement until it can be presented with minimal or no reliance on notes. In particular, the first few minutes of the opening statement should be completely smooth and delivered without any reference to notes, if at all possible. Reduced reliance on notes will also allow counsel to make eye contact with jurors and to evaluate how they are reacting.

Research in advance what the judge's expectations are regarding where counsel can stand during opening, and whether it is acceptable to step away from the podium and move around the courtroom. If counsel does choose to walk during the opening, the movement should be purposeful and not distracting. Counsel should be aware of any nonverbal tics or habits that might be distracting to jurors or might communicate shiftiness or nervousness. Counsel should be very familiar with the rules of the courtroom and facile with all use of visual aids, technology, and documents to avoid any fumbling or distractions.

Almost all opening statements of any complexity will generally benefit from some type of visual aids. Counsel should think carefully about the types of graphics that will be most helpful. As mentioned above, timelines and bullet point outlines of the topics to be covered can be very useful in helping a jury orient itself to the facts in the opening statement. Other good options for opening statements include: (1) documents that identify the key players and witnesses by name, and perhaps with a photo; (2) graphics that explain processes or concepts necessary to understand the case; or (3) photographs or actual examples of important evidence (such as a photograph of an accident scene or a sample of a product alleged to infringe a party's patent). Beware, however, of using too many visual aids or relying heavily on a PowerPoint presentation. Graphics can lose their power when overdone, and counsel can lose his or her chance to connect with jurors if the jurors are busy looking at a screen exclusively, rather than looking at counsel. Most courts require that the parties confer in advance about graphics to be used during opening statement in order to avoid any objections during the presentation.

Karen Kimmey is a trial lawyer and a partner in Farella Braun + Martel's Business Litigation, Insurance Coverage and Intellectual Property Litigation Groups. She represents both large and small businesses, as well as individuals, in a wide range of commercial disputes, with a particular emphasis on class actions, products liability, insurance coverage, and trade secret and patent disputes. Ms. Kimmey frequently speaks and writes about trial strategy and skills, often addressing the challenges that litigation poses for businesses. Her skill in business litigation in Northern California has been recognized repeatedly by Super Lawyers. Ms. Kimmey sits on the board of directors for the Bar Association of San Francisco. She may be contacted at KKimmey@fbm.com.

CHAPTER FOURTEEN

Effective Closing Arguments: The Law and the Craft

Hon. Brian R. Van Camp, Ret.

The vast majority of jurors I've served with are intelligent, conscientious, and careful. Once they've taken the oath, they take their responsibilities seriously. Your closing argument must show them that you do, too. It's hard to overstate the importance of your argument, but bad summations do convert victory into defeat, and good ones preserve close victories.

The Law

James McElhaney, Esq., formerly Associate Editor of *The ABA Journal,* set forth the Basic Law of Final Argument, as follows:

- Don't misstate the evidence or the law;
- Don't argue facts not in the record;
- Don't state your personal belief in the justice of your cause;
- Don't personally vouch for the credibility of any witness;
- Don't argue an irrelevant use of evidence.

"That is the law; all the rest is commentary."

At the risk of embellishing McElhaney's well-stated summary, the "commentaries" hold that you *may* argue from:

- The Law (Jury Instructions) and how it applies to the evidence.
- The Evidence and theories, inferences, or conclusions fairly suggested thereby.

- Damages, as long as you don't add your *personal* belief as to any amount.
- The lack of any evidence, or the absence of a witness (as long as such was only available to your opponent, and only in a civil case).
- The opponent's failure to call an expert to rebut your expert.
- The witnesses' credibility.

You may *not* argue:

- Evidence or facts outside of the record or beyond fair inference.
- Settlement offers or discussions or earlier settlements with other parties.
- Evidence of any subsequent remedial steps taken.
- The "Golden Rule" Argument, i.e., "put yourself in my client's place."
- Any speculation as to what any non-witness might have testified.
- Appeals to prejudice or passion based on a person's race, religion, etc.
- Presence, or lack, of insurance, or collateral sources available, except as allowed by law.

The Craft: How and What You Should Argue

Aristotle teaches that every argument should contain three elements: Ethos, Logos, and Pathos.

Ethos

Ethos—You're ethical; the juror can rely on you. Before your jurors will believe your story, they must *believe in you.* Your jurors want to know who *you* are. Your humanity will be on display; your closing argument will reveal much, such as are you fair? Intellectually honest? Compassionate? Empathetic? What are your values? Do you identify with any larger issues lying beyond, or embedded in, this case, or those universally shared in your community? Are you considerate of their time? Are you well read? Well rounded?

Be precise. When quoting witnesses, jury instructions, statutes, names of parties or witnesses, directions, or locations, do so correctly. With the internet, you no longer need to settle for, "Someone once said . . . ." Instead, get the author's name; it adds credibility and framework. Do whatever it takes to be authentic; it will reinforce the perception that you are diligent and can be trusted.

Be candid. Don't overstate your case and don't ignore the weaknesses of your case. But don't fold in the face of a good argument. If your case has a weakness, bolster it.

Logos

Logos—Your argument is grounded in logic. Marshal your facts. Fit them into the legal requirements of your jury instructions. Latch onto tangential authority, wherever available. Anchor your case to tangible, specific rules and precedents; connect with law, regulations, industry standards or codes, physical facts, or known scientific principles.

Pathos

Pathos—Your argument grips the juror's emotions. You should instill a sense of injustice, if not outrage, over the treatment of your client. Jurors should not only hear, but feel, the justice of your cause. "Without Pathos, no story can be successful"—Aristotle and Gerry Spence, in *Win Your Case: . . . Every Place, Every Time*, St. Martin's Press.

Preparation

"Preparation is the be-all of good trial work. Everything else—felicity of expression, improvisational brilliance—is a satellite around the sun. Thorough preparation is that sun."—Louis Nizer

To organize your **Closing Argument**, Spence advises beginning to prepare the final argument the day you take the case. Make notes of ideas and phrases that come to you when driving, retiring for the night, jogging, reading the paper, seeing a play, or sitting in church or synagogue. Write out whole paragraphs that will work with the jury. Keep a final argument file by your bed, then beside you at counsel table at trial.

- **Tell the story**—The Who, What, When, Where, and Why—especially the "Why." The jury wants to know why they should care about your client. Make your client "worthy"; less so your opponent. Think less like a lawyer, more like Stephen Spielberg. And read *Pixar's 22 Rules for Telling a Story*; see especially Rules 4, 7, 14, and 22.
- **Develop a theme**—Jurors want to know that they're part of a larger picture. Elevate your case to an overarching theme, tying it to a universal truth, good, or value, such as "Individual Responsibility,"

"Corporate Greed," "No One Is above the Law," "Better Safe than Sorry," "Profit Ahead of Safety," "Correct an Injustice."
- **Use analogies**—They can transform the pedestrian into the unforgettable. Get *I Never Metaphor I Didn't Like: . . . History's Greatest Analogies, by* Dr. Mardy Grothe, HarperCollins Publishers.
- **Write it out?**—Yes. Write out your argument, polishing the words and phrases as you rewrite; prepare a "speaking outline," then commit the speaking outline to memory.

The Outline

- Begin with a *brief* introduction. Don't waste time with apologies for your inadequacy or reminders that your remarks are not evidence.
- Open creatively, with an apt analogy, a pertinent quote, an amusing or interesting thing that happened during the trial—anything that lets you smile.
- State your theme, then marshal the evidence that ties the case to your theme, especially inarguable evidence such as physical facts and testimony from both sides that corroborates your argument.
- Appeal to jurors' common sense.
- Discuss the respective burdens of proof of the parties.
- Review and apply the supporting jury instructions.
- "Ask for the order." Tell the jury in clear terms, using the jury verdict, what you want them to do.
- Thank the jurors for their careful consideration.

The Rebuttal

Prepare it first, before you write out your closing. Reverse roles with your opponent, anticipating his or her arguments (by now, you know what arguments are coming).

The length of time for your closing argument should, to some degree, be dictated by the complexity of your case, and certainly, the judge's ground rules or consent. But recall Mark Twain's admonition that "[f]ew sinners were ever saved after the 20th minute of the preacher's sermon." Also, a drill sergeant may get away with incessant repetition, but respect the jurors' intelligence by not belaboring your points.

"Practice, practice, practice!" Your argument will get *exponentially* better with each oral practice. Read it to yourself out loud several times, then record it and play it back. Then practice before colleagues or family members. Ask for feedback, on both style and substance.

The Presentation

Make your words count—use proper grammar. We are a learned profession—sound like it! *The* best book on grammar and style is still *The Elements of Style,* by Strunk and White. Get it, read it, follow it—especially its dictate for brevity!

Your voice is an instrument; use it to your advantage. Work on diction, breath control, and pace (slow down!); observe the pauses called for by your punctuation; vary your pitch, cadence, and volume.

"The body never lies; the body always speaks first."—Martha Graham. Your posture should be comfortably erect; shoulders are back, chest leads to the front. Eyes are "windows on the soul," so make eye contact with each juror as you start and during your argument, but avoid "locking on" to any.

Example:

Sometimes people think jurors don't pay attention. Following every trial, I solicit jurors' written evaluations of all of us, and they are always enlightening. Here are just a few comments on lawyers' closing arguments that I have seen:

- "Her language related well to the jury; didn't use jargon."
- "Should have been more direct; Get to the point!"
- "Seemed a little nervous; not very forceful."
- "Talked too much!"
- "Unsure—not prepared."
- "I liked that he used technology in presenting his argument."
- "Annoying!"
- "Very polished—she'd done her homework."
- "Very professional; humor helped."
- "He talked down to us and wasted our time!"
- "A serious man who addressed his responsibilities well."
- "His demeanor was patronizing."
- "The visual aids, diagrams, & pictures seemed to tell the story."
- "Ambulance chaser! Does not understand how to make things quick—even for an attorney!"

The moral of the story? Never underestimate a jury.

Concluding Counsel

Choose your words carefully, show conviction, study jurors' body language, remind the jury of any unmet promises of your opponent, keep it simple, rehearse with a friend or family, use both reason and emotion—in balance, exude fairness and end on a high note. Your jury will value the hard work you put into your argument, and, importantly, so will your client. *Good luck!*

Judge Brian Van Camp served sixteen years on the Superior Court of California, County of Sacramento, following private practice in business and corporate law. Since stepping down from the bench, he has engaged in the practice of arbitration and mediation. He may be contacted through www.VanCampADR.com.

CHAPTER FIFTEEN

Final Notes on Trial Advocacy from Judges

I, and my guest authors, have covered quite a bit in this area. However, I want to provide a few more notes about trial advocacy, gleaned from interviews with judges and justices over the years.

Golden Rule #1: Passion Is Your Friend

Judges and juries will, presumably, rely more on the facts of the case and the law than anything else, but it never hurts to believe that the trial advocate has some skin in the game—that he or she truly believes that his or her cause is just and that the client's case should prevail. As Jean Giraudoux, the French dramatist, once said: "The secret of success is sincerity. Once you can fake that, you've got it made."

All kidding aside, showing some passion and conviction during the course of your trial signals to the jurors and the judge that you aren't just up there pleading your case because it happens to be your job. Letting your emotions show (in moderate doses) clues your audience in that you actually care about your client and that you believe your case deserves to prevail. As the late United States District Court Judge William Hoeveler explained to me: "I like a little bit of emotion . . . . All things being equal, of course, if a lawyer gets his back into his argument and really feels it, that's a good thing."

When I asked Judge Hoeveler about when it is most appropriate to display this kind of emotion, he didn't hesitate: "The opening statement." He said:

> An opening is not argument, and I have to point that out. But the opening statement is one of the most important parts of a lawyer's offense or defense . . . if it is properly presented, the opening sets the tone and presentation of

the case. While you cannot have argument in an opening, I have seen some lawyers give emotional and heartfelt openings without violating the rule against an argument in the opening. And that's important.

U.S. District Court Judge Paul Huck (Southern District of Florida) agreed, saying:

> I've always felt that if you don't convey to the jurors that you believe what you're telling them, it's not all that likely they're going to believe what you're telling them. It's these little things.

Golden Rule #2: Choose Your Trial Theme Wisely

One of the lawyers presenting the case—either the defense or the plaintiff's counsel—is going to be the one to frame the debate and lay out, in a clear and concise manner, what the issues are that need to be decided. *You* want to be that lawyer—not the other guy.

The way to do this is to develop a strong trial theme—the primary issue over which you will be fighting. If you allow the other side to frame the debate before you do, you risk losing the jury's focus on the issues you need them to understand. Chapter Thirteen, "Opening Statements," goes into this in detail, so I will simply mention a story from one of the judges I interviewed some time ago.

I asked Judge Huck for an example of a strong and memorable trial theme from his years on the bench, and he remembered one in particular:

> I recall a couple of years ago, I was presiding over a trial of a Medicare fraud case. And I had this Assistant US Attorney before me. He steps up for his opening statement and said, "Everybody gets paid." That got everybody's attention. I guessed that was his trial theme.
>
> By the end of the case, I realized what a terrific trial theme it was, because what happened was he talked about every person being paid, everybody involved in the fraud, everybody got paid.
>
> There was somebody who was working undercover. I think it was the money launderer, who was laundering money and bringing cash back to the business. He shows up in the business one day and turns over an envelope full of cash. This is the cash they're going to pay the beneficiaries, because they get paid $100 for the Medicare being used. And he walks into the office. Hands the envelope of cash

to one of the defendants. The defendant turns around and says, "Now everybody gets paid."

And I thought to myself, that is one of the best uses of a trial theme. Because he used it all the way through, and of course he knew where the evidence was going to go. And if I'm a juror, that's going to hit right on the target for me. That was a very good use of a trial theme.

Golden Rule #3: Tell Your Story

And speaking of telling your tory, another universal rule upon which all of the judges I spoke with agree is tell your story clearly, forcefully, and thoughtfully so the judge and/or jury can fully understand your case. Sounds easy, but it is truly one of the hardest parts about being a trial attorney.

You are too close to the case. You know everything (perhaps too much). You are swamped in minutiae. You cannot see the forest for the trees.

Sit down and carefully chart both your opening and closing (allowing for modification to the closing, of course, as the trial continues). Rehearse your speeches with your friends and colleagues. *Demand* that they be honest with you about whether or not they understand you. And get rid of anything that is digressive or immaterial.

Then do your job and get out there and make your case. The judges had a great deal to say on this subject. From United States Magistrate Judge Edwin Torres (Southern District of Florida):

> Lead with your most compelling facts. There must be something about your case that has a story to it. *Don't lead with argument.* Some people tend to get to the legal issues, although you're not supposed to be argumentative. Lead with a story, because that's how people normally communicate. And so, in the concept of "don't tell them but show them," it's the story that then shows them why you're there. The legal stuff comes at the end.

I asked him if by "at the end" he meant the closing. He responded:

> Yes, and even at the end of an opening statement. "At the end of this case, we're going to ask you to find in favor of," whatever it is. But if you lead with your story, then people listen. People will connect with it. Obviously, that's easy to do in a tort case. Little boy is hit by a car. So the first thing out of your mouth is, on this day, a bright sunny day, a little boy went running for the park. He was looking at his ball, crossed the street at the wrong place, and as he crossed, a car hit him at 35 mph breaking his

hip, femur, and leg. All of a sudden, with those facts and that story, the jury is listening. I just made that up, but we're listening, because that's a compelling story. That's communicating.

Judge Huck agrees wholeheartedly:

What I see lawyers, the good lawyers, do (and what the not-so-good lawyers don't do) is immediately give an overview of the case. Right away. So that everything that follows that is put in context. "Why are we here? Why is the jury there? What are the facts to support what you're asking the jury to do, and why leads the jury to come to the conclusion and prevail." And then of course tell them what the jury should do. The key to all of this is establishing a personal rapport with the jurors, a real connection with the jurors. They're willing to accept you as someone they can rely on, someone who has credibility. They believe your story because you are a credible storyteller, so to speak.

People respect someone who does his or her job and tells the story with efficiency and confidence. Be that person.

Golden Rule #4: Use Visual Aids When Possible (but Don't *Overuse* Them)

This issue has been discussed elsewhere in the book when not at trial (see Chapter Nine), but I thought it was important to get the judges' take on the use of visual aids during a trial. Happily, I have found that their opinions mesh with my own. You should, whenever possible, take advantage of the technological innovations that have come along to benefit the trial lawyer, including blowing up exhibits on a big screen, introducing photographs or videotape to the proceedings, and even blowing up selected quotes from a key witness for use in your opening statement.

Judge Huck put it this way:

I found I'm not a real technical person at all. I'm really not. But I've come to the conclusion that today people expect some technology. They expect visual aids. They expect demonstrative aids. They don't have to be particularly fancy or complex, a board is just fine. Also I think you should be prepared to use key exhibits that are going to come into evidence. If you've got a contract with a key provision, have that blown up and read it to the jury. Let them see it in the context of the document, the exhibit itself, or a particularly important business record. You want to show that someone made an omission or some such thing. Obviously, a photograph tells a story. There's no reason to wait until you put the witness on the stand to disclose these exhibits. If you have a good faith belief that they'll come into evidence, most judges will let you use those.

All the same, while PowerPoint is allowed in most courtrooms, it is both encouraged and derided. The exhibits you put up on the screen or insert into your PowerPoint have to assist you, not become the sole means of telling your story. *You* tell the story, not your PowerPoint. As one of the Ventura I interviewed judges opined:

> I allow PowerPoint too, if properly used, it can be very effective. But what I find with newer lawyers is, and I'm doing a criminal assignment now rather than a civil assignment, that the lawyers, new DAs, new PDs, get so focused on their PowerPoint that they lose the point they're trying to make.

All that goes back to *tell a story.* But you've got to do it in a way that's persuasive, and reading what's on the board to a jury is not very persuasive.

The point is: As with everything useful, moderation is the key. Use visual aids and let them help to guide the jury by taking your key facts and blowing them up as big as life, if you can. But do not let the props (or the PowerPoint) tell the story. That's *your* job.

Golden Rule #5: Watch the Clock

Sometimes attorneys think they have to go as long as possible to make their case at their opening statement and closing argument. But this can lead to *endless* openings and closings. Do not make this mistake. If anything, you should attempt to take up the *least* amount of time as possible, yet still get your job done.

Make your points, state your case, and then *sit down.*

Judge Hoeveler:

> All things being equal, of course, a lawyer gets his or her back into his argument and really feels it, that's a good thing. And, of course, being prepared is most important. But he or she should be aware of *how short the argument should be.*

The idea of self-policing—having the presence of mind to know when you are in danger of overplaying your hand—was put succinctly by one of the Ventura judges interviewed:

> And as a practitioner, I think you have to recognize that jurors have an attention span, and that attention span is affected by how exciting what you're saying is, how you're demonstrating it to them, what time of day is it, how close is it to the end of the day, how long jury selection took, etc. All that constellation of factors fits into whether they're going to listen to you or think about when they're going to find time to pick up their dry cleaning. You have to self-monitor. Because if you get to that point where they're saturated, you can keep pouring water into the glass, and the glass isn't going to get any fuller.

I could go on and on to give you other quotes from a multitude of interviews I did with judges and justices that emphasize the importance of being brief and to the point and to then move on, but I think the best way I can demonstrate it is to do it myself.

Golden Rule #6: Know the Rules and Be Prepared

Not all jurisdictions are the same. Federal and state courts all run things a bit differently, some are *wildly* different. I touched on this earlier, but it is worth emphasizing: Know where you are and what the rules are before you proceed.

CHAPTER SIXTEEN

Working with the Media: Getting the Basics Right and Knowing When to Get Help

Greg W. Brooks, West Third Group

Many attorneys will eventually find themselves dealing with the press. Whether it's on behalf of a client or as a spokesperson for your firm or client, today's dynamics—more media than ever and publishers' insatiable appetite to fill screens and pages with content—means it's unlikely you can avoid the spotlight.

As with most things, working with the press goes best when you have a plan, have the information you need on hand, and know when it's time to call for reinforcements. This chapter suggests times an outside professional might make sense as part of the case team, offers a glimpse at the basics of best-practice media relations, and discusses when it's time to bring in the cavalry.

The Basics: Media Interview Rules

The heart of a good interview is simplicity itself: Be informative, aid the reporter, and make the key points you want to ensure readers understand. These general best practices go a long way toward helping make that happen:

- **Get your message across**—Come to an interview prepared with your messages and find opportunities to get them across without ignoring the reporter's questions. Take the initiative. You are the expert. You know what is important to tell the public—so tell them.

- **Be informative, not conversational**—News interviews are exchanges of information. You are the source of that information; the reporter represents the public. Do not feel obligated to maintain the social rules of conduct that guide conversations. Beware of the reporter who remains silent, encouraging you to ramble or dilute your original message. It's human nature to want to fill those lulls with conversation. Don't.

- **Be brief**—Reporters generally don't want lengthy, drawn-out explanations. They're looking for quotable quotes—a punchy line that will fill three lines of newsprint or twenty seconds of air time. Use your twenty seconds to get your message across—there's much more likelihood it will be used. Knowing what you want to say in advance will go a long way in simplifying your answers. Forty-five seconds is about the maximum response time for television and other media as well, unless the reporter truly wants a complete understanding of, for example, neutrino physics—in which case you may have ninety seconds.

True Story:

An attorney I know learned this lesson early in her career in Texas when she was called to comment on a U.S. Supreme Court opinion dealing with state homestead laws and whether or not the feds could trump that. The attorney gave the reporter a long explanation of the law, and then the reporter said to her: so what is your advice for Texas spouses? And she said, "Don't marry a deadbeat." That was the only quote that appeared in the local paper. A sound bite indeed.

- **Don't go off the record**—There is no such thing as off the record. An "off-the-record" comment may not be attributed to you directly, but the reporter often will use the information to confirm a story with other sources. If you don't want something to appear in print, don't say it.

- **Know your role**—When you are conducting an interview, understand your role. If you are serving as a spokesperson for your client or firm, remember: Reporters will not distinguish between personal opinion and your client's position—and neither will the public. Answer questions appropriately. If you don't know the position on a particular issue, find out; don't speculate. If you are providing commentary, opinion, or perspective for a news story, and have not been designated as a spokesperson, make certain reporters understand you are offering your own views as a scholar, researcher, or expert in a field.

- **Don't use jargon**—Avoid using terms or acronyms that can't be quoted without explanation.
- **Avoid bureaucratic language**—"It is clear that much additional work will be required before we have a complete understanding of the issue." Instead, say, "We're working on it."
- **Tell the truth**—The truth may hurt, but lies are deadly. You probably will get caught, and reporters don't forget sources who have "burned" them. Give a direct answer when asked a direct question, even if the answer is "No," "I don't know," or "I'm sorry, I can't answer that question." You will come across as an honest, forthright person.
- **Be patient**—These are reporters, not judges or legal scholars. You may have to begin at the beginning to help them understand an issue.
- **Don't lose your temper**—Sometimes reporters are intentionally rude to elicit a charged response. Don't fall into the trap. Respond politely, in control at all times. Don't get into arguments—your angry comments may be reported without any mention of the provocation.
- **Be friendly**—It's an interview, not an interrogation. Establish rapport with the reporter.
- **Don't (usually) answer a question with a question**—The reporter asks, "What do you think about affirmative action?" Don't say, "What do you mean by affirmative action?" Or, "What do you think about it?" Such responses come across as evasive, pejorative, or hostile. You can use: "What you should be asking is . . . " to redirect the question to a key point you'd like to make.
- **Don't say "no comment"**—Don't say "no comment" or "I can neither confirm nor deny." The public views this as: "I know but I won't say." Instead, tell the reporter that you are unable to comment and, if possible, why. If a reporter asks about a document that is in draft form, for example, tell the reporter: "I'm sorry, this is a working draft, and I'll be able to comment as soon as it becomes public." Offer to let the reporter know when the document is available.
- **Don't answer when you shouldn't**—If you know the answer to a question but can't say, don't hesitate to refer the reporter elsewhere—up the chain of command in the firm, to General Counsel, a judge, or whomever else makes sense and can answer the question.

- Question: "I understand the county is about to be sued for $50 million. Is that true?"
- Answer: "I'm sorry, but I just can't answer that question for you. You could try the County Counsel, but our agency's policy is not to talk about hypothetical legal actions."
- Again, don't answer questions if you are not the appropriate spokesperson. If a reporter presses, repeat your answer. Don't waver. (And don't go off the record.)
- **Don't guess**—If you don't know the answer to a question, say so. And be sure you offer to either find the answer or find someone else who knows. Don't guess.
- **It's okay to make a mistake**—The tape is rolling and you realize you've made a mistake. Or, more likely, you suddenly find you have no idea what you're saying. Stop. Say, "I'm sorry, I haven't answered your question very well. Let me back up." The reporter usually will prefer your new, crisp response.
- **Talk from the public's point of view**—Remember that you are talking through the reporter to the public. How does what you are talking about affect individuals in the community? How does it affect their children? Say it in terms readers and viewers can relate to. If, for example, there was a toxic spill, the public wouldn't care much how quickly it was cleaned up or how many workers dedicated themselves to the effort. The public wants to know whether their health is in danger.
- **Cite facts**—Reporters love facts and figures that will lend credibility to their stories or make certain points. But don't exaggerate facts by using superlatives that make things sound bigger and better than they are.
- **Be prepared to repeat yourself**—Reporters may repeat their question because your answer was too long, too complex, they didn't understand you, or they're simply trying to get a more pithy response. Welcome the question as another opportunity to state your message, perhaps more clearly.
- **Be confident**—You're the expert. You have a message to deliver. Recognize that reporters in fact may be somewhat intimidated by your expertise or position. Put them at ease.
- **Respect the reporter's deadline**—Find out deadlines and return calls promptly. Showing respect for deadlines will go a long way toward building positive media relations. If you can't return a reporter's call, ask a coworker to do so.

- **Don't be defensive**—Make positive statements instead of denying or refuting comments from others. State your message; let others speak for themselves.
- **Be aware of when you are being taped**—In broadcast situations, such as in the studio or when talking to a radio reporter, it is wise to assume that everything you say is being recorded.
- **Use anecdotes and humor**—Use examples to illustrate your points. What will sell a story is not statistics but human interest about real people with real accomplishments. Use humor, an interesting quote. Television in particular is show business, so entertain when appropriate.
- **Avoid reading from prepared statements**—This is especially true when you are on camera. You are the expert and ought to know what you want to say without a "script."
- **Never ask a reporter to preview the story**—Reporters generally never let sources review stories, though they often check back for scientific details. Remember, it's their job to gather the facts and tell the story accurately—to suggest they can't do so without your input insults their professionalism. Besides, they won't let you, so there's little point in asking. It's better to listen carefully during an interview to be aware of when a reporter may not understand something. Remember that the likelihood of your being misquoted is reduced substantially if you speak briefly and clearly.

When to Get Help

Maybe you have a gift for extemporaneous public speaking and a natural command of facts and logic. Perhaps you're even known as a first-rate logician who can cut through to the heart of any complex issue.

In short, maybe you're a badass.

But once the media is involved, you can still get in trouble. Sometimes you need help. Sometimes your client will benefit from having a public relations professional well versed in crisis and litigation PR on the team.

Why? Several potential reasons:

- **Domain expertise and relationships**—Do you know the city editor at the daily newspaper? Or perhaps the assignment desk editor at the local ABC affiliate? If a producer from *Nightline* calls about something you don't want to talk about, do you have the personal history to make the story go away? The popular image of PR professionals having golden Rolodexes and being able to make things go away with a single phone call is overblown. However, the grain of truth is that relationships do matter, and good public relations counsel will have them.

- **Distance**—At times, a hard truth may need to be said or a trial balloon may need to be launched when it would be inappropriate for counsel or client to do so. Having a spokesperson on the team provides some distance. As in chess: If things go badly, it's better to sacrifice a pawn than a bishop.

- **Someone to quarterback the longer game**—In a crisis, dealing with issues in the moment is only the start of the work. Every crisis has a recovery and a road back—elements that certainly involve legal input but are, at their heart, more public facing and dependent on shaping stakeholder/public opinion. Access to outside PR counsel gives the legal team a deeper bench of skills to serve clients or employers not only in the moment of crisis, but in the many moments that follow as well.

And Finally: The One-Minute Media Bible

If you go it alone, keep these fundamentals in mind:

- **Remember the key dynamic that takes place in any interview with the press**—You know far more about your business and its relevant issues than any reporter you will encounter. If a reporter is being aggressive, he or she may be under deadline pressure or (more likely) just covering up a lack of preparation and knowledge. You can use either to your advantage—helping him or her meet a deadline in a timely manner and/or educating the reporter during the interview in such a way that he or she is ready to accept your key messages.

- **Learn to rephrase questions**—Most of the time, reporters fire off questions that are abrupt and, to one degree or another, confrontational. Identify the issue the question raises, rephrase it more to your liking, and then (and only then) answer it.

- **Never take a call from a reporter without preparation**—Always find out who the reporter is, who they're writing for, what the story is about, and what the deadline is. Then, even if the reporter's deadline is in ten minutes, tell the reporter to give you a couple minutes (to take care of a call on another line or whatever) and call him or her back. Take those few minutes to review the key messages you want to get across and how you're going to convey them. Prepare, prepare, prepare!

- **To play up the story**—Humanize it with anecdotes about real people and examples of how an issue or project directly impacts day-to-day life.
- **To downplay a story**—Lean on statistics, numbers, and theory. Complicate it. Remember: Things that lack drama and are hard to comprehend are less likely to turn into a story.
- **Always make a distinction**— between what you think you know and what you know you know. Only talk about what you know you know.
- **Don't lose your cool**—You'll be tempted, believe me. But unless you're at least as well known as the reporter and better liked, it won't pay off. (Presidents can get away with it—sometimes, against an unsympathetic interviewer—but even that can be iffy.) If the reporter is doing something to annoy you (rapid-fire questioning, for example), calmly deal with that specific behavior. "I'm sorry, but I haven't answered your last question yet. Let me continue . . . ."
- **Remember that image *does* matter**—Dark suit. Good posture. Classic tie or scarf. And ask someone you trust to tell you if your breath is bad or your shoulders have dandruff.

Greg Brooks is the founding Partner of West Third Group. For more than two decades, Greg has focused on advancing complex ideas, policies and technical issues to the press, the public, elected officials and stakeholder groups. His career includes strategic communication roles in public relations, marketing, public affairs and journalism on high-visibility projects across the U.S. Brooks' crisis planning and response services, media training and campaign strategies have helped clients win in the court of public opinion on matters as diverse as corporate expansions, nonprofit reorganizations and landmark SCOTUS decisions. Greg can be reached at gregb@west-third.com, http://west-third.com.

Conclusion

Last Thoughts on Public Speaking

Make no mistake about it: **Being a good public speaker is not easy.**

To do the job properly, it takes organization, discipline, a flexible mind, a positive outlook, and the ability to think on your feet. You have to have poise, diction, confidence, brains, and ability. And it doesn't hurt to plaster a big, fat smile on your face every once in a while, either.

But even saying all of that, public speaking is a skill that can be mastered by most anyone.

In the preceding chapters, I have shared with you the advice that I have been able to assemble over the course of my career coaching and working with attorneys, executives, and politicians at every stage of their careers.

I have seen attorneys struggle to prepare for their first cases in court. I have witnessed seasoned CEOs who have had the guts to admit that they could still improve their skills go back to the drawing board and start from scratch. And I have seen fumbling politicians rise to the occasion and motivate an apathetic audience.

But my favorite moments over the years have been watching those who were afraid of speaking before a crowd overcome those fears and discover that they had it within themselves to become more powerful and persuasive speakers.

These moments make it all worthwhile.

I sincerely hope that you will use the tools I have provided for you in these chapters to become the successful public speaker you wish to become. You may not believe that you have it in you, but let me make you this assurance: If you remember AMI,™ if you meet the needs of your Audience, and craft a careful and organized Message, and if you develop an interesting and dynamic Image and Delivery style, you are *guaranteed* to improve.

Never forget that public speaking is a *skill*. And *skills* can be learned—by anyone.

After that, the possibilities—as the saying goes—are endless.

Best of luck!

Resources

Custom Cartoons (as Seen in This Book)

Grace Brooks, West Third Group, graceb@west-third.com. Grace created the custom cartoons in this book and for other projects of mine.

Grace is an author, cartoonist, and a graphic artist with more than 30 years of experience. Besides creating the self-syndicated comic strip "Happily Ever After," Grace's cartoons have appeared in national publications including "The Saturday Evening Post." She is the author/illustrator of the Every Tuesday Girls Club series of books for young adult readers. Grace can be reached at graceb@west-third.com and lives in Las Vegas, Nevada, with her husband and her lovely cat, Senator.

Quote Websites

BrainyQuote.com (my favorite)
Thinkexist.com
Quoteworld.org
Quotationspage.com
Quotegeek.com
Quoteland.com
Bartleby.com/quotations

Books with Usable Stories, Anecdotes, Quotes, and Other Funny Stuff (in Order of My Favorite)

Complete Speaker's Almanac, by Leonard and Thelma Spinrad

This is my favorite. It is organized by date, and for each day there are one or more stories, quotes, and anecdotes about some historical or interesting event. Look up the day of your presentation in this book, and the weeks before and after. See if there is anything in here you can refer to at the beginning of your presentation to grab your audience, and then, of course, circle back to it in your conclusion with some reference to it and your presentation/theme.

I have used it many times.

Speaker's Library of Business Stories, Anecdotes, and Humor,
by Joe Griffith

This is another one of my resources in which I've put a lot of sticky notes throughout. It is organized by topic, not date, and has stories and anecdotes and quotes.

The Public Speaker's Treasure Chest, by Herbert V. Prochnow and Herbert V. Prochnow Jr.

This one is full of amusing definitions, famous lives, quotations, similes, colorful phrases, proverbs, and other useful things. It is yet another one of my resources in which I've put a lot of sticky notes throughout. It is organized first by type of source (story, funny definition, etc.), then by topic. It also has a useful appendix pointing to the right pages by topic.

The Speaker's Sourcebook II, by Glenn Van Ekeren

Like the *Speaker's Library of Business Stories, Anecdotes and Humor,* this book is organized by topic, not date, and has stories and anecdotes and quotes. It is useful when you aren't just searching for a quote, but also want some type of anecdote related to your theme, presentation topic, or point within your presentation.

Oxymoronica, by Dr. Mardy Grothe

This is one of my favorite little quote books, though I've never used any of its quotes in a speech. The author calls it, "Paradoxical wit and wisdom from history's greatest wordsmiths." Even if you also don't use any of the quotes, it's fun to read.

Traditional Quote Books

While these days it is pretty easy to look up quotes by person or topic online (see above), sometimes paging through a traditional quote book works too—and you might even find quotes not on the internet.

Bartlett's Familiar Quotations, by John Bartlett

Indexed by author, these are presented in chronological order by the date of their birth.

I never metaphor I didn't like: . . . history's greatest analogies
by Dr. Mardy Grothe, HarperCollins Publishers.

The Macmillan Dictionary of Quotations

20,000 quotes organized both by theme and by person.

Respectfully Quoted, A Dictionary of Quotations, Edited by Suzy Platt

This is an interesting book—a gem and worth being in any library.

As the editor describes, "for nearly 75 years (as of the time of publication—almost 100 now) members of Congress and their staff have been calling the Congressional Research Service of the Library of Congress to verify quotations they wanted to use in public debate." The Congressional Reading Room staff would do the research and began to compile a file of "quotes that had already been found and to identify those that had already been proved to be either spurious or unidentifiable after reasonable professional search."

Published in 1993, this book is a compilation of the quotes in that file.

This is more than just a book on quotes and lengthy discussions or stories—mostly political in nature—it is a book that documents the original source of the quotes, including dates, where and when first published, and even page numbers. It is organized by subject and contains both an author index and a subject index.

It includes quotes by Supreme Court Justices regarding issues and cases.

Books Filled with Speeches

Sometimes, you just want to—or have to—read the whole speech, not just the quote. Here are several excellent books of speeches, worth residing in any library as well.

The Senate 1789–1989. Classic Speeches 1830–1993. Volume Three. Bicentennial Edition, by Robert C. Byrd

This is a collection of speeches delivered by U.S. senators between 1830 and 1993 and compiled by the staff of the Senate Historical Office.

Great Speakers and Speeches, Edited by John Louis Lucaites and Lawrance Mark Bernabo

As the title says, it's full of great speeches, from the classical to the contemporary.

Contemporary American Speeches, Edited by Richard L. Johannesen, R.R. Allen, Wil A. Linkugel, and Ferald J. Bryan

The Inaugural Addresses of the Presidents, Edited by John Gabriel Hunt

My copy is published in 1997 and contains inaugural addresses from George Washington through Bill Clinton.

The Penguin Book of Historic Speeches, Edited by Brian MacAurthur

Lend Me Your Ears: Great Speeches in History, Selected and Introduced by William Safire

Books about Speeches

Martin Luther King Jr.'s speech "I Have a Dream" is ranked as the #1 political speech of the twentieth century, by AmericanRhetoric.com. John F. Kennedy's inaugural address is ranked #2.

So there is one book I want to mention here. An attendee at one of my "Presentation Skills for Attorneys" seminars told me about it after my program. His son had written it.

Written by Drew D. Hansen, the book is called *The Dream: Martin Luther King, Jr. and the Speech That Inspired a Nation.* This book delves into the history of the process by which King created one of the most famous speeches of all time—as well as how he delivered it. Hansen also analyzes the speech. For anyone interested in this speech specifically, the book is fascinating.

Licensable Cartoon Graphics for PowerPoint Presentations

Mchumor.com (and http://mchumor.com/law-cartoons-pg1.html)
Lawcomix.com
Cartoonresource.com

Paid (and Sometimes Free) Photo Sources for Presentations

iStockphoto, http://www.istockphoto.com
iStockphoto by Getty Images is an online resource for original royalty-free stock images, media, and design elements. It is a site offering vector illustrations, videos, music and sound effects, Flash, logos, and of course, photos.

BigStockPhoto, http://www.bigstockphoto.com/
BigStock is a fast, easy-to-use marketplace for quality stock images. They offer more than 60 million royalty-free photographs and illustrations from talented photographers and artists around the globe, available for almost any purpose.

BigStockPhoto was founded in Davis, California, in the fall of 2004 and quickly grew into one of the Web's leading royalty-free stock image communities.

Flickr, http://www.flickr.com/
Flickr is an online website for photographers and a space to share life's experiences through captured images and video with the world. Its goal is to get photos and videos from its photographers to the eyes of all who are interested as fast and as easily as possible. If you are interested in a photo and would like to purchase it for use at your discretion, simply contact the photographer to negotiate deals and price.

Every Stock Photo, http://www.everystockphoto.com/
Every Stock Photo is a license-specific photo search engine for free photos. They index and search millions of freely licensed photos, from many sources, and present them in an integrated search.

PowerPoint Resources

http://clearpreso.com/

Slide:ology, by Nancy Duarte

Presentation Zen, by Garr Reynolds and PresentationZen.com, garreynolds.com/presentation/sample1.html

http://www.slideshare.net/messierjf/annual-meeting-and-slideumentation-v1

"PowerPoint That Pops," by Kelley Robertson

Countdowns and Watches for Your Computer or Smart Device

Here's a full-screen stopwatch or countdown via your browser—great for timing speeches or audio/video clips: https://www.online-stopwatch.com/full-screen-stopwatch/

You can also find a variety of large-screen clocks, timers, and countdown apps for smart devices in the app store for your device.

About the Author

Faith Pincus is an accomplished and experienced speaker who will boost your self-confidence and give you the tools you need to succeed at public speaking. Faith has trained CEOs, attorneys, elected and appointed officials, candidates, and management at nonprofit associations for more than twenty-five years. As a licensed attorney and former Federal Law Clerk she is also uniquely positioned to understand the speaking skills required of attorneys. Faith's national Continuing Legal Education (CLE) business, Pincus Professional Education, has also provided her with a unique perspective regarding attorneys and others speaking at events and insight provided by hundreds of justices and judges discussing what they expect from attorneys in their courtroom.

Faith has an innate ability to see what works in the public speaking context. She has an unbridled passion for public speaking and for helping people become better communicators. Faith is an expert in the art of persuasion and an accomplished speechwriter.

Current and former clients include Chevron, John Deere, Amgen, Manatt Phelps and Phillips, Buchalter Nemer, the U.S. Department of Health and Human Services, the U.S. Social Security Administration, the American Diabetes Association of California, the American Lung Association of California, the American Cancer Association, the Fair Political Practices Commission (FPPC), Smith Amundsen, Farella Braun + Martel, Commercial Law Litigators Association, and multiple other law firms, individual attorneys, executives, and legal and national nonprofit associations.

Prior to opening Pincus Communications, Inc. and Pincus Professional Education, Faith ran more than twenty-five political campaigns, including campaigns for Congress, the California State Assembly and Senate, and various City and County level seats and initiatives.

Faith previously taught communication at the university level, including rhetoric (persuasion), public speaking, and interpersonal and small group communication. She has published a variety of articles on communication and persuasion, including an analysis of major war announcement speeches.

Faith has a Masters in Communication from the California State University at Fresno and a Juris Doctorate from the University of Iowa. She is a former Judicial Law Clerk for the Honorable Oliver W. Wanger of the United States District Court, Eastern District of California, and a Member of the Order of the Coif. Faith litigated for one of the top AmLaw 20 law firms before creating Pincus Communications, Inc. and Pincus Professional Education.

Faith also owns Finz Case Law Updates, a monthly audio analysis and summary of published appellate opinions in California, which began in 1992 by Steven Finz.

Faith Pincus is located in Los Angeles and can be contacted at faith@PincusProEd.com or (877) 858-3848. For more information about her professionally recorded *Being Heard: Presentation Skills for Attorneys* and *Public Speaking Made Easy* (for non-attorneys) DVDs, see www.PincusProEd.com or www.SpeechAdvice.com.

Index